ENABLERS CAN KILL ADDICTS

Bob and Ann Wilson
With Dr. Michael K. Haynes

ISBN 0-9772472-051495

Printed by
AMA Nystrom Printing/Finishing
920 North Valley Mills Drive
Waco, Texas 76710
Printed in the United States of America

Dedication to Nellie Meadows

On May 21, 2005 Nellie Meadows went to be with her Lord. She passed away following a short illness with her family by her side. As has already been stated in the contents of this book, without Nellie there would be no Meadows House. She left a legacy that few people ever leave. She began a ministry work that will continue to change the lives of young men until Jesus comes back to claim His children. There is really no way to calculate how great an impact her support for this work will have. When one life is changed it affects literally thousands of others for generations to come. Meadows House has already been instrumental in seeing numerous lives changed and set free from the bondage of addiction. Because of Nellie, families have been reunited and fathers are now taking their God given responsibility to their homes and communities. Nellie Meadow's presence will be profoundly missed.

Nellie and her boys from the Meadows House Faith Based Treatment Program

Enablers Can Kill Addicts
By
Bob and Ann Wilson
With Dr. Michael K. Haynes

Introduction — The Tale of Two Worlds

Introduction

Enablers Can Kill Addicts

"It was the best of times, it was the worst of times, it was the age of wisdom, it was the age of foolishness, it was the epoch of belief, it was the epoch of incredulity, it was the season of Light, it was the season of Darkness, it was the spring of hope, it was the winter of despair, we had everything before us, we had nothing before us, we were all going direct to Heaven, we were all going direct the other way . . ." The Tale of Two Cities, by Charles Dickens.

The tale of two cities embodies the multifaceted and complex problems of addiction that has invaded our homes, families, children, workplaces and churches. In the drug world, everyone uses some sort external chemical stimuli to change the way they feel. In the respectable world no one uses illicit drugs for any reason. In the drug world most everyone has been incarcerated at one time or another. In the straight world no one has ever been in jail or prison, or for that matter, hasn't even seen the inside of one. In the drug world time, reason and order are not a part of the thinking process and very few things make any sense. In the law-abiding world, logic, thought and consideration cause things to make sense. In other words, the drug

i

using world and the world that doesn't use are poles apart – daylight to dark; black to white. The non-user not only does not understand those who are addicted, they don't want anything at all to do with them until the 'them' becomes personal.

These two worlds very seldom touch or intermingle knowingly. Addicts do go to church or are found in the workplace, and the members of the church or co-workers may have family members who are addicts or alcoholics, but for the most part there is very little communication due to a complete lack of understanding of what the dynamics of addiction really are. Because of this, everything is covert or secret. The straight population does not know nor would they even believe the things that go on in the under world of chemical dependency. It is a huge sub-culture that is sweeping America like an out of control Nevada forest fire leaving lives and families in total devastation.

In the following pages there are some suggestions for how to bridge the extremely wide gap between these two completely different populations. The church and family members need to know how to help those who are trapped in the throngs of addiction without doing more harm than good. Somehow, these different realms must begin to learn something about one another so that true restoration and recovery can occur on both sides. The user inevitably leaves hundreds of hurting people in the wake of his or her quest for their drug of choice. Then, there is the other side of the coin. There are the family members or friends who have been repitiously lied to and manipulated by the abusers who are sometimes just as wounded by a totally different set of issues. All too often, the loved ones of addicts have just thrown up their hands and walked away from them or kicked them out because of not knowing what to do or how to help. Then they stand on the sidelines and painfully watch their sons or daughters; their fathers or mothers; their brothers or sisters spiral downward until the end result becomes either incarceration or death.

Such is the story of Bob and Ann Wilson and their son Tom. Bob and Ann have been Christians most of their 41 years of marriage. They were in church almost every Sunday and raised their children to have the same belief system. Only recently were Bob and Ann forced to live out the nightmare of finding their 38 year-old son was heavily addicted to methamphetimine and had been for well over 10 years before they were aware that such a thing even existed. They were clueless about the drug world and thought Tom's erratic behavior was coming from character flaws.

Tom, a former professional bull rider, started his use of 'meth' in order to keep up with the hectic schedule of owning and operating a dairy farm, which required hard and long hours without a break. Methamphetimine is speed and speed kept him going. Being an extraordinarily obsessive compulsive personality, he took to the drug instantly and chased the dragon until the dragon himself finally turned and breathed fire through out the entire family from the grandparents down leaving nothing but ashes and pain when all was said and done. However, this is a one in a million story that has such an incredibly powerful ending that it must be told so that hope can be released possibly affecting millions in both worlds.

What has happened in the Wilson family can best be described as an obvious intervention of God. There is really no other explanation for how things that were so horrific for so long could turn out for such good so quickly. That doesn't mean that scars are not still present and some things won't ever be the same as they were before drugs entered the scene. But, God is at work healing even those. This book will help countless numbers of hurting parents as well as users to understand that enablers can kill addicts if they allow their negative consequence behavior to continue or support it in any manner. We hope to keep people who are in this trap from giving up and walking away simply because they do not know what to do. It is the combined prayer of Bob, Ann and Tom Wilson, as well as myself that this book of basic prevention and intervention principles will help solve the overwhelming drug problems that families are facing daily. We deeply desire that the pages become worn. Enablers Can Kill Addicts is destined to become a useful tool kit for those in the snare of addiction and those who are forced to watch the destruction because of their enabling behavior.

Dr. Michael K. Haynes

Airing Dirty Laundry
Chapter One

Bob and Ann Wilson were abruptly introduced to the quagmire of the criminal justice system when they heard the piercing words announcing the judge, "All rise!" Neither was prepared for what was about to take place. The courtroom was cold and featureless. They both stared at the back of the head of their 38-year-old son, Tom, as he stood with his lawyer to face the bench. They had never been in a court of criminal law before – especially sitting behind their oldest child. After being seated, everyone watched the judge look over the pages of charges against him. The silence was almost deafening except for the occasional rustle of paper. Tom Wilson had been a methamphetamine addict for the past 13 years. Not knowing anything about the signs of addiction and what to look for, his dad knew something had gone drastically wrong with him, but he thought it was just a terribly flawed character. Bob and Ann, like many parents, were clueless about Tom's problem or what the world of chemical dependency was all about. His probated sentence for previous drug related charges was in jeopardy. In the case prior to his, a young man received a 15-year prison sentence for offenses far less than Tom's. Everyone was scared!

Tears began to swell in Ann's eyes as she thought, "How did this happen? What did we do wrong? Why did we not see what was going on right before our eyes?" As she caught quick glances around the room she saw Tom's daughters, her granddaughters, sitting behind their daddy waiting for someone to speak. Finally, it came! Tom and his lawyer stood.

"Mr. Wilson, you have tried probation and come up lacking. The charges against you are somewhat involved and I see no other course of action other than to revoke your probated sentence and send you to a Substance Abuse Felony Punishment program at a unit in the Texas Department of Criminal Justice to be announced at a later date when a bed becomes available. You have shot your last wad with this court and we hope this will help you to get your life straightened out."

The reverberating sound of the gavel came down sharply on the hard wood and caused Bob and Ann to jump sending waves of confusion and nausea through them both. Their son was going to prison. Everyone stood as the judge left the courtroom. What they had just witnessed during this surreal setting was completely foreign to them. They knew nothing about drug use or prison programs for the people who abused them. They were stunned! Tom's family gathered around him as the deputy put handcuffs on his wrists and prepared to take him to jail. The tears that had just swelled up a moment before escalated to obvious weeping. This could not be happening was the expression clearly showing on everyone's face. What were Bob and Ann going to do this time to get Tom out of the situation he had gotten himself into? They had always been able to cover for him and had done so because that's what parents do. No matter what the situation had been, Bob had tried to be a good dad. However, he was completely in the dark about where to turn or what to do this time. The feeling was utter helplessness.

The family began to slowly file out of the court building almost in a daze while a few of their supporters and friends who had been praying for Tom and the hearing gathered around them speechless. The Wilson's had just undergone the most drastic shock of their lives and no one really knew what to say. When they finally got in their car to return home, Bob and Ann both slumped in their seats and with long heavy sighs they just looked at one another. The shock was wearing off and a deep and threatening depression loomed like gigantic storm immediately off shore. Tears unashamedly and silently rolled down each of their faces.

"What now?" Bob whispered and turned his head.

"I have no clue," responded Ann.

"I don't know how to get him out of this one," Bob continued.

Ann just stared out the window with the customary thousand-mile stare that accompanied true and heartrending trauma. "I guess it's simply up to God now," she spoke softly shrugging her shoulders slightly. "It's out of our hands."

"Well, I don't accept that. There's bound to be something we can do," Bob reacted.

Driving home, Ann's thoughts once again started racing through her mind competing for a place at the forefront. Only this time, they were much more intense. "No, this can't be happening! Surely they aren't really going to send him to prison! Didn't the judge see that he had family who love him right there in the courtroom? We will get him through this! We always have! His two daughters were crying and holding on to him while the deputy was trying to put handcuffs on him. How can they be so cruel? Don't they have a heart? How did we get here? How could it have gone so far? We have always been able to bail him out before. The judge wouldn't even listen this time. They didn't even give him a chance to go change his clothes. I wish we hadn't told him to wear dress shoes. Now what? He is 38 years old.

Images from Tom's playful youth began to flow like a perpetual fountain.

 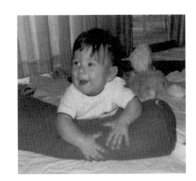

Tom at the ranch as a baby

She couldn't believe how time had passed so fast. Where did it all go? Now, his life is in shambles. He is divorced – his family torn apart. His addiction to methamphetamine has stolen 13 years of his life. Thirteen years and his children are 16 and 12 years of age. How does he make up for all the lost time of seeing them grow up? Those years are gone, as well as most everything he has ever owned – all sold – little by little to support a drug addiction. I cannot believe it. Why didn't Bob do something? Why didn't I? We thought his life was going so well. He was married and had a family and had settled down on his grandparents ranch that he had loved since childhood. He had dreamed of living there since he was a child. Her mind reflected on that beautiful farm.

Tom at the Ranch in Evant, Texas

He began designing his dairy and his grandparents helped him build it. He had so much to look forward to. He seemed so happy." Finally, her mind began to slow down before it short-circuited.

As Bob and Ann pulled down the ally to enter their garage, they passed the driveway of Dr. Michael Haynes on the opposite side. They had only seen him on a few occasions because their houses faced different streets. Nellie Meadows, Ann's mother and Tom's grandmother, lived on the same street as she did and her garage faced the same alley. Ann made a mental note of Michael because in the back of her mind she thought he might be some sort of counselor. She got out of the car and went on about her day about trying to stay busy. Bob went to his upstairs office to ponder the events of the morning and to try to think of a way he could get his son out of the complete mess he had made of his life. He did not understand why or what had caused Tom to become addicted to drugs, of all things. Time seemed to stand still as he tried to think about what he could do. His first move after coming up with nothing but a jailbreak was to get to his computer and get online. He hit search and typed in the word 'methamphetamine.' He was instantly drowned with so many sites he could not believe his eyes. "Whoa!" he said under his breath after becoming even more confused. "I never knew this stuff was such an enormous problem. Why have I never heard of it?"

You see, Bob and Ann Wilson were in church every Sunday morning and evening. Bob taught an adult Sunday school class. They were very faithful and had been close friends with many of their pastors over the years. All of their connections and support base was either with church friends or work relationships they had developed before retiring. Neither one of them would have recognized chemical dependency if it had been staring them in the face. It just wasn't a part of their world on a personal level. For thirteen years they saw what they thought was only unpredictable and unbalanced conduct on the part of their son. Tom had starting riding bulls on the professional rodeo circuit and that shocked them enough.

After he could no longer ride, he began to raise bucking bulls for the circuit. Tom had become a master manipulator and could fool even the closest people to him. He was such a good schemer and deceiver; he could often times fool himself. He had a great personality and on the surface was well liked by almost everybody. Not thinking much about it, a friend introduced him to 'meth' and he started his use after opening the dairy farm and trying to keep up with the hectic schedule. He had never experienced anything like the feelings he had when he used 'meth'. When he was high he thought he could conquer anything that the planet threw at him. It was like he was truly a king! Consequently, early on in his addiction, he used more and more and more and more often until what he was using began to use him and he was hooked. He had gotten deeply and quickly involved in an entirely new world.

'Crystal meth' is an extremely fierce form of speed and is powerful enough to call you in the middle of the night even if you don't have a phone. Because of Tom's obsessive-compulsive behavioral patterns, he was a perfect candidate for the unrelenting clutches of this particular form of illegal drug. Here we have a perfect example of the tale of two cities. You see, in Bob and Ann's life no one did drugs. However, in the life of their son, Tom, everybody did.

The night was long. Neither Bob nor Ann could sleep. They were both wondering about what went on inside of a jail or prison in this day and age. Everything that had seen on TV and in movies was horrible, and their oldest son was right in the middle of the madhouse of the universe. What might have been said was long since over. Ann heard a slight snore. She looked at the clock. 3:48. She began to softly pray for her son. "Lord, I remember when our family was young and I guess I thought we would always be. We were so close and knew each other's ways and problems." She thought back to when the kids were little and how much she could influence them as a loving mother.

Ann and Bob Wilson, Trisa and Tom

She continued praying. "Now, it seems I have no control at all. I feel so helpless. You have opened my eyes to a small part of the pain and the struggle in an addict's life. I asked you to lead me to where you wanted me to serve. I asked you to give me a heart to serve You, but Lord, this is not what I expected. This is a world so foreign to me. A world I have never before been exposed to. Thank you Father for sparing me that. However, it is a world my son has been living in and in order to help him, I need a quick education and I don't know where to get it. You have answered my prayers and have set some things in motion that can save Tom's life and make him whole again. Father, show me what You want me to do. Use me. I am your servant. If this is where I am to serve, give me guidance." She turned Tom over to her Lord Jesus and in the blink of an eye, she drifted.

When Ann woke up God's leadership had come to her during the short night. She knew what she had to do. She heard Bob in the kitchen.

"Bob," she said as she slipped behind him. He jumped. "I am going across the ally this morning and talk to Dr. Haynes. It seems to me that he is some sort of a counselor. He might know how to give us some direction."

"Ann, you know how I feel about airing the family's dirty laundry!" His voice was unwavering.

"This is not a normal family circumstance, Bob," she confidently replied as she opened a diet coke. "I don't know why, but when I woke up God told me to go across the ally and talk to Dr. Haynes. So, that's what I'm going to do."

Bob knew that she would follow through with it and resolved himself to the idea. "Well, I don't want to be around when you do that. Anyway, I need to find out when and how and even if we can see Tom. I'm going to run over to the jail," he replied without looking at her. Little did he know that his son was trapped in a system much larger than anything the Wilson family had ever dealt with in their entire lives.

Bob backed into the ally and went the opposite direction so as not to have to pass Dr. Haynes' driveway. As soon as he left, Ann looked up the Haynes' number and picked up the phone. She quietly prayed, "Lord, please do not let me make a mistake. Seems like I've made so many lately."

She took a deep breath and dialed. Michael's wife, Marj, answered the phone. Looking at the caller ID she thought Ann was another and older Wilson that lived up the alley and wondered to herself why she would be calling her. When Ann introduced herself, Marj realized who she was. She asked if she could come over and Marj told her that the back gate was open and to come on. She prayed ever step of the way and knocked on the Haynes' back door.

"Come in, Ann." smiled Marj as she opened the door. She invited Ann to sit in the living room.

"I know you're wondering why I am here. Let me get right to the point. Bob and our family have a problem and have no inkling what to do." Then Ann began to tell Tom's story. She couldn't help but cry. Marj listened to her intently.

About half way through the conversation, Marj interrupted and said, "You need to talk to Michael."

"I know, that's actually why I came," Ann replied.

"He is on his way home."

No sooner had she uttered the words than she heard the same back gate open again and Michael came in through his study. Marj met him.

"You need to come to the living room," she whispered. "Ann Wilson who lives behind us needs your help."

He put his case down immediately and went through the hall. "Hello Ann," Michael smiled and stuck out his hand as he entered the room. "What's up? How can I help you."

"Dr. Haynes, we've got a problem," Ann shared. "Please call me Michael," he said. They all sat down and Ann began to tell the same story she had shared with Marj only this time she brought in more details about Tom and his problems. She opened up and shared for over an hour. It was good for her and Michael just listened as she ventilated which was something he knew she needed to do. Afterward, he asked her to wait a moment until he made a call. When he had heard the part of the story about Tom's probation being revoked because of his drug use, he made a call directly to the probation office. He had already been working closely with probation and parole for a couple of months because Texas had stopped funding the drug treatment programs inside the prison units due to budget shortfalls, so he had a working relationship with the community supervision attorney and director. He found out what he needed to know about Tom and returned to the living room where Marj and Ann were waiting.

"Ann, oddly enough, I am working on a faith-based treatment alternative out patient program with the Bell and Lampasas counties. I just called a good friend of mine who is an attorney for the department and he looked up Tom's situation for me. I'm going to run over to their office and visit with them about your son and I will get back in touch with you this afternoon." Michael continued to fill her in on his new curriculum and what the state was doing to try to solve the problems of cutting out some of the treatment programs in the prison system. "Let me go to the garage and get you something to take a look at in the meantime," he said and left.

He came back in a few seconds with several video tapes and some booklets about 'meth' and other drugs and their effects. "Ann, a long-time friend of mine and I wrote and produced this material over the past several years. It could be that you and your husband don't know how drugs have become such an enormous problem in America since as far back as the '60's." He told her what to watch first while she was waiting on him to get back from the probation office.

"You hit that right. We know absolutely nothing about drugs, except what we have been told that once you're an addict your always

will be." she faintly smiled.   "We have never faced anything like
yesterday in that court room in all of our lives."

"Well, I have good news for you Ann," Michael smiled back.
"Jesus Christ can change an addict's heart and give him or her a brand
new life. Someone has misled you. Your son *can* become drug free.
The medical model engrains everyone with the fact that once they are
an addict they always will be, but that is simply not true when Jesus
enters the picture."

As Ann was walking back through the alley, it was as if the
weight of the world had been lifted from her shoulders. "Thank you,
Father," she said out loud. She felt hope for the first time in months.
"I did the right thing," she thought.

When she got home she went straight to VCR and plugged in
the tape. Bob had come back since she had been over at the Haynes'
and she excitedly told him about the visit. He could literally see and
feel her sense of relief and restored hope. "He's actually been working
with the probation department! He left to go there just a few minutes
ago! He wants us to look at some of these videos while we wait for
him to come back. He said he would come over here later this
afternoon. He and Marj are very nice people."

"Well, we can't see Tom today," Bob replied. "So, lets start learning something about this mess," referring to the drugs.

Both Bob and Ann had always been quick studies. But now they were hungrier than ever to know more about what they were going to face in the future. It was hard to accept, but they had already discussed that they could not change the past. They turned on the player and sat down without hesitation.

The usual music and movement of a well-produced film was at the beginning. *"Many families will have to cope with friends or family members who abuse drugs," the moderator of the tape said in a deep voice. "However, the parents, spouses, friends, and children of those who are dependent on drugs share a tendency to deny the problem."*

They both looked at each other at the same time. "Bob, this is exactly where we went wrong," Ann spoke up lifting herself to the edge of her chair and putting her face in her hands so that she could watch and listen more intently. Due to the differences in their personalities, it was easier for her to admit that they had enabled Tom and had probably been in denial through the entire course of his life. They had always been there to get him out of any situation he had gotten himself into because they truly loved him and thought this was the way it should be done.

The speaker was a huge black man dressed in a very colorful jacket. He continued, *"Things may seem to get better, or people may justify the situation for a variety of reasons. Denial can turn into a downward spiral for both the users and the people who love them. While placing the blame on the one who is involved in substance abuse, the family often fails to realize its own dysfunction of enabling. The recovery of a chemically dependent person is nearly impossible without the cooperation and recovery of the family as a whole."*

Bob was feeling a little uncomfortable with where he thought the tape was leading. He had always prided himself with being a good father and provider. However, there was no way around the fact that this was addressing the problem at its very core. He knew it down deep but didn't really want that knowledge to surface. Ann, on the other hand, was into it and there was nothing she wanted more than to find out how they had totally missed seeing Tom's real problem.

The video continued, *"While no one would knowingly contribute to the destruction of someone they love, certain attitudes and behaviors actually do just that. One of the greatest priorities in freeing the dependent individual is to identify and assist those who are co-dependent and addicted to the addicted person. Every chemically dependent individual has one or more well-meaning friends or family members who unknowingly assists them in maintaining their destructive behavior."*

The Wilson's were off and running on a completely different journey than they had ever experienced in their over 40 years of marriage. They both knew in their heart of hearts that God was preparing them for something far greater than they could even imagine. They just never really sought what that might be. Bob had surrendered for the ministry at 14 years of age. He had always known that he had a spiritual calling on his life, but he had tried to run away from that or ignore it ever since then. Being unusually talented, he had been able to almost escape. Now – he was hemmed up in a corner and he truly knew it was God that was doing the hemming.

As the tape continued, Bob got up and got a yellow pad without taking his eyes off of the speaker. *"Parents, teachers, and friends may sometimes justify what the user is doing by looking beyond their actions. In other words, it's easier and more comfortable to overlook or ignore. However, it is dangerous for anyone to overlook the obvious signs of drug use, drugs or items related to drug use. Sometimes it's the secretive behavior of an addict or those they hang out with that give them away. People who are enablers often have fear that a confrontation may jeopardize their relationship with the abuser, or create unpleasant conflict. Consequently, they simply discount the abusers actions or assume the wrong thing about abuse. Enablers often have no clue about drugs, so they misjudge their destructive power to destroy the entire family.* **Rationalizing to keep from dealing with the truth is never constructive."**

Bob's mind was already on overload and this was just the first tape. The big man continued as he looked straight into the camera and right into the Wilson's spirits. *"Parents who search for an excuse for their kid's behavior by blaming the school, church, friends or parents can easily find one. No school, church, friend, or parent is ever perfect, so the family can easily blame other family members, teachers, preachers, or friends, thus causing further division. This merely encourages drug use by taking the focus off of the real problem . . . the abusers themselves. Out of pain and confusion, families often seek a "scapegoat" to help them feel less responsible for the problem at hand.* **Remember, blaming never heals.** *Parents often excuse contradictory behavior even when they discover drug abuse because they don't want to embarrass the family. Denial is fueled by the myths. Any mood-altering drug is a dangerous drug. Any drug use must be responded to with appropriate and enforced consequences. What moves an abuser to action are consequences and accountability. Don't be guilty of loving or helping someone to* *death."* The tape faded and went to black by drawing closer and closer to the speaker's eyes.

Bob and Ann felt numb. Had they inadvertently come close to killing their son? Although the speaker didn't actually say it directly, the message that rang loud and clear was that **enablers could kill addicts.** This was the first time they had been made truly aware where the problem might have come from. They had been denying enablers. Tom had been wearing a mask. They had all been wearing masks. Nothing was real – nothing but the present circumstances. They just sat there in silence for at least 5 or 6 minutes. Then, Bob got up without speaking, put his hands in his pockets and slowly walked to the back window of the den. The room was spacious and the plate glass windows were two stories tall. He looked out over his back yard, which was full of huge oak trees, and without turning around said, "This was a very serious thing, Ann. Why did we not see it?" He verbalized his earlier thoughts as he continued, "How could we have been so stupid?"

"I don't know," she said choosing her words carefully. She knew what he was feeling and wanted to make sure he didn't take these events too personally. Bob was a high 'I' personality type and criticism was not a good thing for him. Nor was not being carefree and

outgoing.   "I believe we just need to learn all we can about what's
happening. Not necessarily what has happened," she spoke gently.

"I know.   I'm not going to beat myself up too bad," he
whispered knowing what she was thinking. He could see Dr. Haynes
roofline from where he was standing. "Things could have been worse.
I guess."

"I wish we could have seen this material before all of this came
to the surface so that we might have known what we were dealing
with," she said looking through some of the books.

"We wouldn't have been ready to listen to this stuff!   And,
anyway, I thought you said you didn't want to look at what has already
happened," said Bob.

"That's true, but we might be able to help somebody else who is
in the same boat with their kids as we have been."

He turned and just looked at her. He thought about how she
could see light behind the dark clouds most of the time. He didn't
always know how to get behind the darkness. But, like her, he knew
the light there. They made a good team. "Want to watch another one
while we wait?" He glanced at his watch.

"Sure," she responded. "

Bob and Ann Wilson were brilliant people and loving parents,
but what they had heard in their limited scope of the drug and alcohol

world was that once a person was an addict, they would always be an addict. Basically, people of the secular mindset had told them that there was no cure for their son.

Now, they knew better. Hope is such a powerful thing. The Wilson's despondent spirits had been lifted. Even though they knew in their minds that God would never desert them, they sometimes felt He had. They felt like they had been stumbling around in some mysterious, sinister, dark cavern for the last few months. But today, all of a sudden, a small tiny ray of light had pierced the darkness and caught their eye. It was high and far out of reach from where they were standing, but they found themselves being drawn by its power and they knew exactly Who it was that was doing the drawing. God had not deserted them! They turned to Him immediately and determined to learn all they could about the world of addiction so they could be used by Him to help Tom and possibly thousands of others who were facing this terrible life-controlling problem. That very day they mentally enrolled in a crash course about drugs and their effects. They started gathering all of the information they could find. Their late fees for the course had long since been paid.

The Drug Free Family PAK

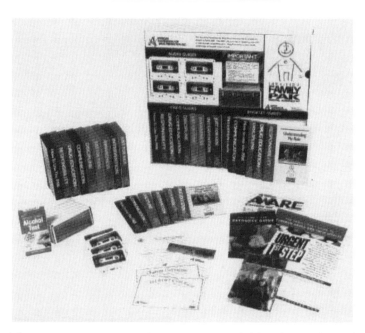

The Drug Free Family PAK is available through Bob Wilson Ministries or The Faith Based Counselor Training Institute. This incredible tool contains extensive information on how to equip your children to walk safely through a drug-infested society.

The Dragon Breaths
Chapter Two

What we are never changes – our family, our children, our DNA, or our parents. Who we are is in a constant state of change from the day we are conceived until the day we die. For most people the changes are simply life's movement of ups and downs. However, for Bob and Ann Wilson the changes over the past 13 years had been nothing short of radical. They owned a beautiful home in what they thought was a quite little innocent town. Not too large and not too small – a good place to live and raise kids and grandkids. It looked like 'Pleasantville' on the outside should someone simply drive by. However, behind closed doors things in their family had become painstakingly insane. Nothing was as it ostensibly appeared. Everything was in total disarray. Their supposedly organized tidy lives had been slowly thrown into an utterly chaotic downward spiral of confusion because of their son's drug abuse. The enemy of their souls had crept in so subtlety that no one really saw him coming. To be sure, there were numerous signs, but no one actually knew what they were seeing or what to look for.

It was not supposed to be this way at Bob and Ann's age. Retirement was in order. They had worked for this stage all of their lives and it was what they had thought they had earned. Just kicking back and spending time traveling and having an occasional visit with the grandkids are what they had planned for and what was supposed to happen.

As Bob and Ann were about to plug another videotape that Dr. Haynes had loaned them on How To Recognize When Your Child Is On Drugs, the doorbell rang. They both instantly jumped anticipating the possibility of good news that might be waiting on the other side of the door.

"Its Dr. Haynes," Ann turned and called to Bob in the den as she opened the door. "Please come in. Did you find out anything?" Ann said anxiously.

"Yes, I found out quite a bit," replied Michael calmly so as not to shock her.

Bob came to the door from the den and stuck out his hand. "I'm Bob Wilson, Michael. I've seen you in the alley but I don't believe we have formally met. Please sit down and tell us what's going on with Tommy. Did you get to see him?"

"I did, Bob. And I will share everything I know 'cause I'm sure you're worried. But, I need to visit with you guys personally before I do that. Do you have a little time?

"Sure – please," said Ann. "Absolutely," answered Bob almost simultaneously. "Come back and sit down."

Michael could read their eyes and body language. They were truly frightened and he knew he needed to choose his words very carefully. He could tell right away that they had never been in this kind of situation before. They sat down and he began to share only some of the things he had found out about Tom, his probation, his charges, his numerous dirty urine analyses, and his missed opportunities for recovery, his probation officers, his file and everything else he knew they wanted to know. He had been able to acquire most of the information he needed to determine the depth of the predicament the Wilson's were in.

"When did you first find out Tom was using methamphetamine or speed?" Michael's words were even and gentle. He had been a counselor for over 30 years and he knew this family was treading where even angels might fear to tread. Prior to entering the counseling field, Michael had played music professionally and was personally and intimately familiar with chemical dependency. But, he knew that he was on very thin ice because what he had uncovered over the past few hours about their son was not good at all. He also was quite sure that Bob and Ann had no clue as to how critical and how deep Tom had been caught up in the dope world. In fact, it really couldn't have been much worse. The tentacles of the criminal justice system were sunk very deeply into their son and he didn't want to cause the Wilson's any more difficulty or pain than they had already experienced.

Tom's Probation Card

"Do you want the whole story," asked Dr. Haynes. Bob winced trying not to let it show. He had never been one to make personal things public, so to speak. Especially when they were bad and humiliating.

However, Michael noticed Bob's look and asked, "Let me be straight with you guys and ask a simple question. Do you want my help? You don't know me and maybe there is someone else you would rather call to help. But, you are for sure going to need someone knowledgeable about what is happing here. If you want me to get involved, tell me how much."

Bob and Ann looked at each other and then Bob said, "We don't know where to turn or who to turn to. We love our pastor but we haven't even told him about this problem. Sometimes, it's hard to go to church when others know your problems, you know? However, I am sure he would tell us that we should find a good Christian counselor who was familiar with helping people who have addiction problems. I guess that's how we would answer your question. We don't know what else to say."

"If you can't help us," Ann chimed in, "maybe you can point us in the right direction to someone who can."

"Again, let me be completely honest. There are not many people who know how to deal with the dynamics of addiction – especially with people who have 'crystal meth' problems. The established treatment industry, by that I mean, the secular or worldly programs in the jail or prison systems don't work. They are simply revolving doors for addicts to play games with the system and the entire process is based on sheer economics. Those are just the plain and documented facts," continued Michael. "If I work with your son, I will have to look him in the eyes and see if I can determine if he is really ready to 'own his stuff.' I want to be at least partially convinced that he wants to get his act together and take responsibility for the way he has messed up his life – and above all of that, I want to further determine if he is ready to make a lasting change. I am a faith-based counselor with years of experience in working with this population of miss-fit toys and I know personally and experientially that the root problems that cause addiction are spiritual. I don't mean to sound unkind, just truthful. Tom might not be ready to admit that. But, until he is, there will be no permanent change in his life. The State or incarceration cannot change the heart. Only God can do that. Prison can scare people into not wanting to come back, but it cannot give them a new life. A person has to be looking up to see bottom before they are truly ready for that type of transformation. This kind of change means death to yourself, your own agenda, your desires, your personal goals and dreams, your everything so that the life and purpose God has designed for them to have can come forth."

Bob and Ann were silent, but they were tuned in to what Michael was saying. They knew this was the truth. They had heard sermon after sermon about the cost of following Jesus as Lord. But, now, it had dropped into the slot. Their only fear was that Tom might reject that kind of approach. At least, he hadn't listened to them in a number of years. If fact, he usually became intensely angry when they brought up the subject of God or church. However, under the present circumstances they didn't really have much choice.

"Dr. Haynes, we are both Christians, and have been since we were children, and we have raised our kid to believe in Christ. And, we honestly believe they both do, " said Bob. "We go to Taylor's Valley Baptist Church. Our pastor is Jeff Loudin. We recently began to realize that the only way Tommy would ever wake up to the truth would be to lose every thing he had. That has happened. It is embarrassing for me to even talk about it. I'll be the first to admit that I tried to keep these things hidden to save face for our family. But, we love Tommy and we know he is in a world of hurt."

Then Bob and Ann began to share the disgusting details of how all of the problems with Tom started. "You know, Michael," Bob shared. " I once read that the devil sometimes comes in the back door of our homes unnoticed, undetected and even unseen. Then, all of a sudden, one day he is right in our faces screaming and demanding to have what he thinks he owns. This is just exactly what has happened to Ann and me. We knew absolutely nothing about drugs. We had never heard the term 'meth or crystal or ice.' We were as blind and naïve as any two parents could have been concerning what Tommy was into."

"I know this might not be comforting, but there are literally thousands of parents in that same situation," said Michael

"Let's just give you a brief history of Tommy since high school," Ann entered the discussion. "Bob, jump in if I leave out something you think might be important."

"Well, Tommy starting riding bulls when he was in high school," related Ann. She continued, "We lived in Odessa for years and then moved to Lampasas. We couldn't sell our house in Odessa, so we got an apartment in Lampasas and Tommy lived there for most of his senior year while we went back and forth trying to sell our property and move. We didn't know about the bull riding until sometime after he started. Tommy has always loved us with all of his heart, and he didn't tell us because he thought we would panic. He was definitely right!"

Tom Had Become a Champion

"I thought he had lost his mind!" laughed Bob. "Bull riding of all things. Football was bad enough. He played for Odessa-Permian. He was looking at getting crushed every time he took the field. Friday night lights, you know!" Bob recognized that it was the first time he had laughed since the court hearing. Michael was a good listener and easy to talk to.

"Me too! I couldn't believe it," Ann snickered too. "As a mother, and a timid one at that, I was in shock! I just knew he would get hurt or maybe crippled for life or even killed. But, as time went along, we watched and learned about bulls and rodeo and discovered that Tom was a very good rider. By the time we moved back to Lampasas, he had developed quite a reputation in the central Texas area."

"After high school, Tommy went pro and began to travel the professional rodeo circuit. He was never at home. He traveled all states and even Canada. He later married, but he was still always gone. Even after his first child was born, he was still continuously gone," said Ann.

Bob chided in, "We knew that was no way to raise a family, but there was nothing we could say to change his mind and, really, he was doing what he wanted to do, so we thought he was happy. If the truth be known, that was what we had always wanted for him – to be happy."

Michael asked, "Was he making a living? Most people I have known who have tried that didn't do so well financially."

"Not really," Bob answered quickly. "We were always paying rent, bills, payments, or buying groceries or something all of the time." Michael just looked at Bob and Ann without expression, but they knew what he must have been thinking. Enablers par excel lance.

"Anyway, no. He wasn't," said Ann. "Tommy could always pull the wool over our eyes and make us believe everything was all right. He was constantly in and out before we knew what the real issues were.

"What do you mean, in and out?" asked Michael

"Well," Ann continued, "Tom lived in his own world and everything was always about him. If it wasn't about him, he would create some kind of a crisis so it could be about him. Every Christmas or holiday was a nightmare. In fact, we often thought of spending Christmas in Hawaii just to avoid the fights that would inevitably occur. But then, there was Trisa, our daughter, and all of the grandkids, both Tom's and hers. So, we just prepared ourselves, but we sure dreaded those times that were supposed to be so good. We just thought this was the personality he had developed from the rodeo or whatever. He was gone most of the time, so we really didn't know what was going on with him."

"Then came the dairy farm," added Bob. "This is when he really started using illicit drugs we found out a few months ago. He was 26 years old. He had retired from riding bulls and he and his granddad, Ann's dad, went into a partnership of buying and selling stocker cattle. Tom could convince us that anything he wanted to do would be successful and we went along. Really, he had wanted to do that since he was a kid."

Tom and Granddad

Tom, Trisa and their Granddad Royce

"Was that Nellie's husband?" Michael asked. "I want to put all of the pieces in the right place." He knew that Ann's dad had died, and he had seen Nellie in the alley talking with Marj. Marj and her mom and dad had known the Meadows from Marj's hometown of Goldthwaite. "It's a small world," Michael thought to himself.

"Yes," said Ann. "That was my dad, Royce, Tom's granddad. But that's a whole other story we will get into if you began to work with Tom. That relationship will help you to understand much of what we think is going on with Tommy right now."

"Anyway," Bob picked up the conversation, "the stocker cattle endeavor didn't go fast enough to suit Tommy and he had been talking to some of his friends in the dairy business. They persuaded him that he could make a bunch of money in a dairy and he bought into their persuasion."

"Yeah, literally, bought into it," said Ann.

"We'll get to that in a minute," Bob interrupted, "I don't want Michael to know how blind we really were just yet."

"Oh well, we might as well get it out and get that part over with," he continued. "There were oil leases in the family from Royce and Nellie. We had some shares as well. We were in good shape and had the money to set Tommy up in the farm. Little did we know at the time that we were setting everybody up for financial and personal disaster? We were all making it possible for our son to fail big time."

"That's called enabling," Michael said softly. Bob and Ann just stared at him for a moment as if they had never made that connection. "Go ahead, " Michael said with his hand resting on his forehead and chin.

"Well, there is much more to the story, but the up shod of it is that over the next several years Tommy lost everything he had and part of what we had set aside for our own retirement. He could always talk us into his schemes and plans, and we just kept pouring more and more money down a dry well, as we say in the oil business."

"And all of this time, we fought and argued," said Ann. "We didn't have an inkling of what was going on in his head. But, we knew something terrible was wrong. We tried to blame his wife, his work, his friends, his kids – everything but us! We knew that we were good parents and would always be there to catch him if and when he fell or failed."

"Michael," explained Bob, "much of this began to come home to me when I went to Tommy's house one day and found him asleep on the couch when he should have been out working. I got furious and we had a knock down drag out. I got right in his face and yelled at him about being lazy and to at least think about his kids. I told him that God had given him his daughters. He raised up and looked at me with wide eyes that were blood red. He said that he and Kelly had made his kids and God had nothing to do with it. He told me to get out and then he lay down and went back to sleep. I just stood there and looked at him. Then, I slowly looked around the house. It was a filthy mess. I knew that we didn't raise him to live in that kind of filth, but it still never dawned on me that drugs were involved. I left the house that day with tears and fear. I thought I had come face to face with a demon in my own son. I now know that that is exactly what I had seen. But I didn't know then."

"When Bob came in," said Ann, "he was as white as a ghost. He was ashen. I was horrified and asked him to tell me what happened, but he said to give him some time. He went up to his office and didn't say another word. There was nothing I could do but pray. So, that's what I did. Finally, he came down and told me all about what had happened."

"Then things began to quickly fall into place," Bob whispered. "We found a bag of meth on our bed. He lied and said it was someone else's. Of course, we believed it. Then he got stopped and busted. He said it wasn't his fault, and again, like fools, we believed it. Then came the probation and we blamed his friends for getting him into trouble with the law. And on and on. It was always everyone else's fault but ours. You used the term enablers. I guess we were classic enablers," Bob finished as he had begun – with a whisper.

Michael had listened for almost an hour and a half. Then he said, "Guys, you have every right from a human viewpoint to be beating yourselves up, but don't do that. It won't do either of you any good. You cannot live in your memory because there is nothing you can do to change what is in the past. You absolutely must live in your vision. So, we need to deal with what is now and what is to come. And, on top of that, there is nothing you could have done to fix Tom. Only Tom can make the choice to fix Tom. And without God in the picture, he most assuredly cannot fix himself. You will hear things about addiction being a disease that can never be cured. But that is not true. That is a medical model that has become what the secular treatment providers and counselors believe. However, we both know that God can give Tom a new heart and a new life."

By this time, both Bob and Ann were silently crying. What Michael was telling them was nothing new; they had just never seen it in this perspective as it applied to their son and his addiction. But they had already entered a crash course on drugs, their effects and how to recognize the signs and symptoms that they had so blatantly missed or denied.

"Bob, in the drug world there is a term called 'the chase of the dragon.' When someone gets high for the first time on crack cocaine or methamphetamine, it releases all of the stored up endorphins in the brain and it feels like you can literally conquer the world. It is a far greater feeling than anything a person can ever experience. This even includes sex, which is God's highest intended pleasure for man." He could see agreement in Bob's eyes as he glanced at Ann. "However," he continued, "the high doesn't last long and once it happens, a person can never reach that level of high again. They try, but they can't. The brain will never again produce the number of endorphin neurotransmitters that were stored up and released. I will explain all of this to you at another time, but trying to reach that type of high again is called, 'the chase of the dragon.' Some people overdose trying to reach that original high and they die. I am afraid that Tom has been chasing the dragon for close to 13 years. It is also apparent to me that the dragon has finally turned and breathed fire throughout your family leaving nothing but ashes and pain. Where we go from here is up to Tom. He is very fortunate that he is not dead, and by all rights should be. A drug overdose happens every 9 minutes to someone in our country."

"Wow!" exclaimed Bob. "That is exactly what has happened," echoed Ann.

"If I am going to work with Tom, I will need to meet him and I will need to do that this afternoon. You are not aware of the mess he is in and I am not sure I can do anything about it as far his probation being revoked and him going to jail. But, you had better brace yourself for just that. After I talk with him again and see where his head really is, I will tell you what I have found out from the powers that be and whether or not I need to get involved or refer him to some friends of mine that are very good in this area."

"Can you see him soon?" said Ann, and with that the two-hour conversation drew to an end.

"May I make a suggestion?" Michael said holding up his hand. "Watch this next videotape so that you will at least know what you are looking for if and when you do get to see him. I taped this off of an ongoing series concerning how methamphetamine is taking over the drug world for many different reasons. You guys need to know what you are up against. Tom already knows, but he more than likely doesn't know what to do about it. To further my suggestion, get yourselves educated! I will go back to community supervision and visit with them since talking to you. I can give them a better read as to the family support Tom has."

They reluctantly agreed and popped in the video when Michael left. It was Dr. Haynes teaching in his school, The Faith Based Counselor Training Institute.

Dr. Haynes teaches on the Dangers of 'Meth' at an FBCTI School in Houston

The music started and the title faded in,

METHAMPHETAMINE: The Crack of the New Millennium!

As Bob and Ann sat down to watch, the moderator came on with his introduction – pictures, kids and all. This was a news story, not something that was a teaching tape or a theory or conjecture. It was reported and revealed as fact. He was exposing what had been happening under the surface in America for over 20 years. They were slack-jawed when they saw the images and heard the stories. This was the life of their son. They could not keep the silent tears from flowing even though they did it privately and in silence.

The speaker continued, "What the fast food industry did for eating-on-the-run, crack did for cocaine use in the 80's and 90's. Crack's low cost and wide availability combined to introduce the drug to tens of thousands who might not otherwise have been able to

afford to flirt with cocaine. It spread through the inner cities of America like a raging forest fire devastating everything in its path. Crack was the 80's and 90's "superstar" drug problem. Rappers rapped about it, preachers preached about it, and the media hammered it for every headline it was worth."

The tape moderator was on a roll and the Wilson's were glued to the screen and on the edge of their chairs.

"It was like crack or rock was everywhere all at once. Springing from the inner city street corners, it moved across the country like a contagious plague, showing up on campuses and playgrounds, and spawning thousands of fortified, fortress-like "rock houses" where addicts wallowed on the floors in stupored states of high. Crack earned the reputation with users as a cheap, almost instant high. However, non-users considered it to be one of the most dangerous drugs ever to hit the streets. It was responsible for a virtual tidal wave of drug-related crime and an incredible surge of new drug treatment programs.

In the 80's and 90's, crack had everything going its way. It was highly addictive, easy to manufacture, and provided a high profit margin for dealers. However, it had one weak point for it's North American distributors – dependence on South American growers and powder cocaine suppliers. The coca plants from which cocaine is produced will not grow in our climate.

However, there was a new "superstar" drug that was patiently waiting in the background to take its place at the forefront in following the new millennium. Enter methamphetamine. Meth, as it is commonly called, carries a "made in the U.S.A." label. In the same manner as crack swept through the inner cities in the 1980's, and 1990's, methamphetamine has recently hit rural America like a wrecking ball. You see, unlike crack, meth is not derived from a plant. It contains only chemicals that are readily obtainable from an almost infinite variety of sources. All that is needed is a manufacturer who is commonly referred to as a 'cook'."

The pictures were vivid. Bob and Ann were in a state of shock because they had seen scenes identical to this in their own presence. They just didn't know anything about what they were looking at.

"Meth," the tape continued, "is produced in clandestine laboratories located mostly in rural areas. These "clan labs" generally contain an assortment of hazardous and volatile chemicals creating major health and environmental problems as they are usually discarded illegally or just abandoned by the 'cooks'. This is much easier done in an outdoor setting where old wells,

waterways, ponds, lakes, open land, and public sewer systems are found. However, the production has progressed to anywhere and everywhere.

Small towns have been particularly vulnerable to meth labs due to two primary factors. Number one, people in rural areas have bought into the lie that all drugs are done by inner city youth. There is an extreme state of denial in these smaller communities that anything like the scourge of illicit drugs could ever happen in such a "Mayberry" type of setting. And number two; they usually do not have consistent or adequate education and exposure to drug prevention programs that deal with things like this type of easy access production. The internet is full sites that show the details of how to produce all sorts of things that can kill our kids in a heartbeat or the blinking of an eye."

"Bob, how could we not have known about something so widespread? Why didn't Trisa tell us? Why didn't someone tell us?" Ann was furious.

"Trisa did," he said silently. "If you'll just think back, she tried. We just didn't listen or didn't want to."

"Simply put," the speaker repeated, "most people in smaller towns would not have the street savvy to recognize the

*manufacturing paraphernalia if it were spread out before them.
Denial and ignorance leaves the door so wide open that "cooks" can
set up a lab in the house next door, the local motel, or virtually any
storage facility available. Thousands of manufacturers are moving
to the country for that very reason.*

*One central Texas county sheriff recently reported that the
drug trend in his county could be summed up by one word –
methamphetamine. At this point, most of the meth was made to be
shipped out, but the boom of meth is faster than anyone can
quantify, and rural young people are being seriously affected by the
current trend continues."*

"Rural areas are where most of meth is made," Bob thought.
"Man I didn't see that one coming!"

*"Other rural areas have told of meth-related arrests
increasing 1,100% over the past five years. Law enforcement officials
have announced that methamphetamine is much more aggressively
harmful than the vast majority of other illegal drugs. "Meth
eventually will lead to paranoid psychosis, violent behavior, theft
and murder," a police officer said on the tape.*

Then the video began to teach. It began to tell what the signs
were and what to look for if a person was addicted to meth.

46

What Are The Effects of Methamphetamine

"Methamphetamine may be trendy and cheap, but methamphetamine is death," reported a recent AP article. As a powerful stimulant, meth, even in small doses, can increase wakefulness and physical activity, and decrease appetite. Oral ingestion or snorting produces a long lasting high that continues for as long as half a day. However, along with these seemingly advantageous traits, the drug has numerous dangerously toxic effects. In high doses meth can elevate the body temperature to lethal levels, as well as cause convulsions. Because of the extreme psychological addictive power of methamphetamine, a cessation of use will result in compulsive drug-seeking activity. In one recent episode, a New Mexico man beheaded his 14-year-old son and threw the head from his van onto a highway because he had run out of his supply of meth.

In addition to being addicted to meth, chronic abusers exhibit symptoms that include violent behavior, anxiety, confusion, and insomnia. They also display a number of psychotic features, including paranoia, auditory hallucinations, mood disturbances, and delusions. The paranoia can result in homicidal as well as suicidal thoughts.

Short-Term Effects Include:

➢   *Increased Attention*

➢   *Decreased Fatigue*

➢   *Increased Activity*

➢   *Euphoria and Rush*

➢   *Increased Respiration*

➢   *Hypothermia*

Long-Term Effects Include:

➢   *Dependence*

➢   *Addiction*

➢   *Psychosis*

➢   *Paranoia*

➢   *Hallucinations*

➢   *Mood Disturbances*

➢   *Stroke*

Meth is an equal opportunity destroyer. Because it can be produced by performing a simple chemistry procedure using over the counter cold remedies that contain the ingredient pseudoephedrine, labs can be set up in bedrooms, garages or even the back seat of a car. In an article from a 2002 Arizona newspaper entitled "Meth Epidemic is Spreading to Households," the story was told of a 3 year-old boy who fell asleep on the couch in his mother's apartment and later died after being overcome by the fumes from methamphetamine production in an adjoining room.

Some say that the rapid growth of this devastating drug is due to the huge profits that are easily gained. A novice can get into the meth business for less than $150 and produce an ounce that will sell for $1,000 to $1,200 on the street. One law enforcement official said, "We're kind of surprised that people in neighborhoods aren't more outraged by the number of labs out there. In addition to the danger of explosions, the residue creates very serious environmental problems. There needs to be more awareness."

Awareness Includes the Following Suspicious Activity:

> *Strong chemical odors from areas nearby*
> *Chemical containers being stored about property; vehicle*
> *Heavy short term traffic to and from suspected location*
> *Power cords being run from a residence to an outbuilding*
> *Gasoline generator running late at night*

Methamphetamine is commonly known on the street as, "meth", "speed", "crank", "crystal", and "ice." It can be snorted, smoked, injected, or ingested. Users include the broadest possible assortment. They come from a variety of age groups, lifestyles and geographical areas. They range from curious teens and college students attracted by the drugs' reputation for increasing energy and sexuality, to truck drivers and shift workers who use the drug to stay awake for extended periods of time to judges and lawyers who are in charge of the criminal justice system.

*No community, small or large is safe from "the crack of this millennium." In order to combat the epidemic abuse of methamphetamine, along with the dangerous meth labs and their hazardous ramifications, community involvement is of paramount importance. By taking the time to report suspected drug activity in your neighborhood, just one person can make a difference. The tape closed and faded with the speaker saying, **Enough is Enough!***

"Bob, I want to say it out loud once more just to let it sink in! How could we be so blind to what was so obvious?" asked Ann in a dazed and coarse tone.

"I'm tired of asking that question, Ann," Bob replied back almost before she had finished her statement. "I like what this guy said – enough is enough! We need to get off of our blessed assurances and get in this fight! This has almost, if not already, destroyed our son's life! There must be other parents out there just like us!"

Bob and Ann Wilson had found what God wanted them to do and had begun their ministry.

Turn Your Eyes On Me
Chapter Three

As Michael was pulling into the parking lot of the probation office, his attorney friend and the director were coming out of the building. He looked at his watch and it was almost noon.

"Hey, Dr. Haynes. How is it going with your client?" asked Tim. Tim was the lawyer for Community Supervision, commonly called probation, who had been working with Michael on the new program for the inmates coming out of the drug treatment programs in Texas prisons. Both he and the director were excited about what had been accomplished over the past couple of months, so Michael had a good relation with them and they were the decision makers as to Tom Wilson's immediate fate.

"That's what I came to talk to you guys about. When do you think we might have a short sit down?" he asked.

"You're welcome to go to lunch with us," said the director.

"Great, I'll just follow you." Everybody agreed.

There was nothing but light conversation as they went through the buffet line at the Chinese restaurant across the street. They ate quietly and finished with a cup of hot tea.

Michael began the serious part of the discussion. "As you know, I am trying to work with a young man that you are very familiar with, " Michael cautiously stated.

"Yes we are and it doesn't look good for him at all, Dr. Haynes. Especially with the judge he has," said Tim.

"Let me briefly tell you how I became involved with this situation," responded Michael. "I visited this young man in jail for a short time yesterday. His parents live across the alley from me. Our garages sort of back up to one another. I came home a couple of days ago and his mother was in my living room crying. She related her and her husband's story to me and I felt compelled to try and do something – at least for them."

"Well," said the director, "This boy is quite a problem and has been for some time now. I don't see anything we can do at all. He is definitely going to go to the Substance Abuse Felony Punishment program in some unit somewhere whenever they find a bed. And, that could take up to 15 weeks."

"I completely understand," said Michael, "but, does he have to stay in jail until that time. I mean this is a perfect opportunity to see if what we have developed program wise will work. Plus, he has an excellent family support system and maybe I could do something with him even prior to his going."

"I don't know, Dr. Haynes. We have never done anything like that before. Plus, there are several other people involved. Not just us. His probation officer for the most part," said Tim.

"I know, Tim, but Texas has never done anything like shut down the therapeutic programs for drug rehabilitation in the units before either. If we are going to try what we have been working on, it might be far better to find out if it works now on just one person than to wait until 400 are dumped on us." Michael pled a good case.

"Call me later," said the director thoughtfully, "and we'll let you know. I need to talk to his PO, but you may be right."

"OK, about what time?" said Michael as they stood to leave. "Let me buy your lunch?"

"Not on your least," said Tim. "Not after all you have done for us. Make it about 4:00 pm."

While Dr. Haynes was trying to get Tom released from jail and placed under his care, Bob and Ann were digging into the material he had left for them to begin their intensive study on the substance abuse problems that faced virtually every family in the world.

"I'm going upstairs, Ann," said Bob, "and look the Signs and Symptoms book over. Maybe this can give me some clues as to what we should have been looking for and didn't see."

"OK, I'm going down to mom's and visit with her and pray," replied Ann as she walked out her garage door for the journey two houses down. As she passed Michael's driveway on the other side, she whispered under her breath. "God, please give him favor and strength with whatever he is trying to do for Tom." She could hear her mother's garage door opening.

Bob got comfortable and sat down to read. When he did, the following words literally became alive and leaped off the pages at him. The first thing he noticed was the name of the author. Michael K. Haynes, Ph.D. "I can't believe this guy lived right behind me and I was too proud to ask for help," he thought. "This is the first thing I would like to tell parents if I ever get the chance – get off of your duffs and stop your denial. Quit thinking this can never happen in your family or to your kids! And quit being embarrassed to ask for help!"

SIGNS AND SYMPTOMS OF SUBSTANCE ABUSE:
By Michael K. Haynes, Ph.D.

Beginning at the Beginning

*The first step to being able to understand and trust the signs and symptoms of abuse is to have some awareness of **why people do drugs in the first place.***

The basic causes for people doing drugs are in the lives of every person. Everyone is vulnerable who does not know how to cope with loneliness, boredom, stress, anger, and fear or peer pressure. All of these things are very prevalent in our society. People initially use substances to change the way they feel or to handle a feeling they don't want to sense. This could include anyone at anytime.

It is also important to understand, however, that the reason(s) an individual initially uses drugs may not be the cause of their continued abuse of substances. Initial use may be for pleasure, acceptance or relief. But, continued use turns to abuse when the drug forces the body or mind to demand its continuance. This is called a psychological or physical demand.

People who use substances to escape or deal with the pressures of life may learn the hard way that, for many...You do drugs, and then drugs do you. When that is the case, the addicted individual does develop a severe problem that needs assistance. They are not bad, evil or unworthy of our concern. But, they are dangerous in society and cannot be tolerated. As they lose control in their addiction, they become more and more dangerous to those with whom they work and live. The earlier the intervention, the better the chance for recovery is.

Of great importance is the fact that as a "crisis user" or "recreational user" continues to use, it takes more of the drug or the use of a more powerful drug to reach their high. More of the drug leads to more dysfunction and more signs and symptoms. While a user may be functional early in their use, they will eventually "act like the drug." Our goal is to intervene as soon as possible for their sake. Mood alteration is Mind alteration.

"So that is what I saw when I confronted Tom and thought I was looking into the face of a demon," thought Bob. He continued to read.

How Does A Substance Abuser Look And Act?

When drugs are in the brain, behavior changes. The parents or family members are usually the first to see this change. You are the one who has the most contact with the person and can spot declining performance that may be caused by a substance abuse problem. Physical and mental impairment from drugs or alcohol can easily be seen in someone's appearance and conduct.

"Right! Easy if you know what you are looking for!" whispered Bob to himself.

All too often, however, enablers are reluctant to make judgments based only on opinion. Nevertheless, opinion is what counts. The one's who are closest opinion is the basis for "just cause" or "reasonable suspicion" for some confrontation about what might be going on in their loved one's life. Just to let it go in order to avoid a conflict can cause a person to fall deeper into the throngs of his or her addiction. When a parent, family member, or friend knows the person's baseline behavior, it is not difficult to recognize impairment in behavior or performance.

Baseline behavior is the excepted behavior you anticipate from your history with an individual. Any uncontrollable, erratic movement or changes may signify substance abuse or some serious medical condition.

Bob heard Ann come through the garage door and called for her to come upstairs. She must have been gone for a couple of hours, but he didn't notice the time. He had made some copies of the sections he thought might be the most important to them and he asked her to sit down and read. Ann was a student at heart, but she was particularly interested in this material because it was so personal. She immediately began to look over what Bob had copied.

"Did you see who wrote all of this stuff?" she exclaimed.

"Sure did!" Bob replied. "We might could have saved ourselves a bunch of trouble had we known. However, it is the future I'm interested in – not the past." They continued to plow through the information devouring every little fragment.

Trusting Signs and Symptoms

How can you trust the signs and symptoms of substance abuse? Why are they used as key detection tools? Quite simply, drugs impact the body by impacting the brain, and the brain changes behavior. When a person is angry, you can tell. The body language is obvious. When someone is sad, it is easy to spot. These are normal human moods and are demonstrated in behavior. Drugs cause abnormal mood changes - abnormal in the sense that they are externally induced. The chemical user is seeking some sort of mood alteration. However, as we have stated, mood alteration is mind alteration. Just as you can read a person's mood by observing them walk, talk, and interact with their environment, so you can read the effects of chemicals on the brain. You can trust the signs and symptoms because drugs work! They will change the chemical nature of the brain and thus change behavior. It will happen every time. It is consistent!

When the chemicals take control, the user loses it. Their behavior is now consistent with the way the drugs impact the brain and body. Those who watch need to be able to recognize the effects that certain drugs have on the way a person behaves. Drugs cause baseline behavioral changes to the degree that the user becomes out of control and a danger to themselves and others. This is the time for action on the part of those who love and care for the user.

"My word, Ann! Look at this. I have never heard of such things! But, there it was – right in our own back yard!" Bob finally began to understand.

"I know," Ann nodded. "Look at the signs that were so obvious. Trisa tried to tell us. Even Kayla tried. They must have known so much more than we did. But, Bob, maybe we didn't see because we simply didn't want to see!"

"Well, don't you think that goes without saying, Ann? Just listen to this! One of the ways to recognize drug use is rapid changes in someone's moods! Does that fit Tom or what?"

"I sure does," replied Ann, "we never knew what to expect, but I never once thought about drugs. At least I don't think I did."

Rapid change in mood.

The user may go back and forth from being uncooperative to cooperative, quiet to talkative, sad to happy, confident to anxious, calm to jittery, trusting to suspicious, and so forth. The reason may be that between the "down" mood and the "up" mood.. If the mood swings in the opposite direction, it may indicate that the effects of the drug are wearing off.

Weight loss and loss of appetite.

Nervousness might appear along with other habits such as starting to smoke or increasing an existing smoking habit.

Reluctance to show the arms or legs.

If a person is taking drugs intravenously, he or she will try to hide the injection marks by wearing long-sleeved garments even in the heat of summer or wearing slacks in place of skirts and dresses. Bloodstains on sleeves may appear.

Withdrawal symptoms.

The user may show the physiological effects of a drug as it is wearing off. The common symptoms are: a runny nose, sniffling, red eyes, trembling of hands or mouth, unsteady gait and a general tiredness. Sometimes they may sleep for days at a time.

"This is like reading Tom's autobiography," sighed Bob. He felt totally defeated and inadequate to deal with thinking about what he and Ann had allowed to happen to their son without getting him some help. But Bob Wilson did not give up easily on anything he put his hand or mind to. Neither did Ann. They were just being overwhelmed with a sunamia of information they should have been open to learning about in smaller portions years before. The Wilsons, like thousands of families, never believed this scourge could ever effect them or anyone they cared for. Neverhtheless, their love for their son drove them further into the abyss of the drug world to learn all they could learn without experimenting themselves. That, of course, was never an option. They continued studying most of the rest of the afternoon waiting on Dr. Haynes to return.

Symptoms of drug effects.

The user will usually show signs of being under the influence. Generally, a drug will either relax or excite. A person who has taken a relaxant (depressant) tends to be slow moving, dreamily happy, and likely to talk with slurring of words. The person who has taken an excitant (stimulant) tends to be energetic, twitchy, fast moving, and likely to talk in a rapid and non-stop manner.

Possession of a drug without permission or reason.

Drugs can be in the form of prescription drugs or illegally manufactured drugs. They might appear as pills, tablets, capsules, powders, pastes, leafy materials, gum-like substances, and liquids.

Drug Paraphernalia

Possession or concealment of drug paraphernalia, such as a syringe, needle, cooker spoon, roach clip, glass pipe, etc.

Sores and Scarring

Needle marks, boil-like abscesses, scabs and scars, especially on the arms, legs and backs of the hands.

Lethargy

Drowsiness or general lethargy, especially when accompanied by scratching of the body to relieve an itching sensation. This suggests an overdose of an opiate drug.

Change in mood.

The opiate user may vacantly stare and be generally unaware of surroundings; the stimulant user may be excited, happy and talkative; the user of marijuana, inhalants and depressants may be sleepy; and the user of hallucinogens, like PCP and LSD, may engage in bizarre and possibly violent conduct.

Change in the size of eye pupils.

The pupils will greatly constrict immediately after taking an opiate. The pupils of an amphetamine user will dilate.

"Ann, do you remember how many times we commented about Tom's wild-eyed expression? Read this," Bob handed that page to her.

Change in eating habits.

The abuser of stimulants will go for long periods of time without eating. The narcotics user may have a loss of appetite or consume candy, cookies, soda pop, and sweet-tasting food items.

Illness symptoms.

For example, the opiate user in withdrawal may have the sniffles, flushed skin, muscular twitching and nausea; the user of hallucinogens may experience an increase in blood pressure, heart rate and blood sugar, irregular breathing, sweating, trembling, dizziness and nausea; the cocaine user may have inflamed nasal membranes.

Pro-drug Attitude

The use of drug jargon, awareness of how drugs are administered and their effects, and an attitude that excuses or defends drug use. The possession of magazines or literature that are marketed for persons interested in substance abuse is another indicator. Constant cell phone use is another current indicator. Text messages especially.

Financial Problems

Addicts will have a discrepancy between income and expenditures for necessities. Addicts will spend most of what they earn (and steal) on the substances they crave. They have a constant need for money. This may appear as borrowing from friends or family, stealing, writing bad checks, or any way to obtain money. They will come up with elaborate plans for impossible endeavors. If they have enablers around them who do not recognize what is happening in their lives, they are at great risk to lose everything – even their lives.

"I can't take any more of this," Bob spoke under his breath. "Ann, we need to show this to our pastor. He needs to understand what is happening to our family."

"I thought you wanted to keep it to ourselves," said Ann with a quizzical glance. She knew it was time to come out of the closet. For a truth, they were already out of the closet, but they had really not talked about it to anyone but Nellie and Dr. Haynes. They didn't know what to say, but they were definitely in the most difficult school they had ever experienced about a subject they were beginning to not only passionately hate, but also fiercely fear.

At 4:00 pm sharp, Michael called the probation office and asked for Tim. He immediately came on the line. "Dr. Haynes, how are you doing?" Tim always sounded like you hadn't seen him in months.

"Any news?" Michael asked.

"Well, Dr. Haynes, he responded. "There is good news and bad news. The bad news is that there is no way Mr. Wilson can get out of going to the SAFP program. But you do know that the sentence time has been cut from 9 months to 6 months?" Michael listened without comment. "The good news is that the director, Mr. Wilson's probation officer and I agree that he might be a good test case for the program we've been developing."

"So – exactly what does that mean, Tim?" Michael spoke evenly.

"Well, that simply means he can be under your counseling on a daily basis with regular visits to his PO and random but regular urine analysis'. I want you to know, Dr. Haynes, that this is a first for this office. I have never seen it done before in my tenure with the State of Texas, or anywhere else for that matter. Mr. Wilson can get out of jail in the morning and report to you sometime tomorrow. It will probably take 12 to 15 weeks for a bed to become available in the

SAFP facility, wherever that might be. We won't know until the time comes. If it weren't for this decision, he would have to remain in county jail until that space became available."

"Sensational!" Michael tried not to sound too blown away. "That's great, Tim. Tell everyone we will do the best we can, with God's help of course, to help this young man get his life turned around. His parents and family will be thrilled. I don't know how to thank you."

"I want you to know that we all will be watching this project. If this works, you will certainly have to gear up for a bunch of folks," Tim finished. "You stay in touch now," he said and hung up.

Michael held the phone to his chest for a few seconds before cradling the receiver. He really didn't know if he was ready to become involved in what had just been explained to him and what he had opened himself up for. "I've gone too far with this to back out now," he thought. "What if it doesn't work? What if this boy really doesn't want to stop the dope?" "What if…what if…" A thousand of thoughts swirled through his mind.

Dr. Haynes and his wife Marj had founded a counselor training school called The Faith Based Counselor Training Institute in 1997.

Marj and Michael

Dr. Haynes Basic Course Max Lucado's Church San Antonio

Previous to that, due to insurance companies and managed care, he had been fortunate enough to sell his part of a private counseling practice in Dallas and get out before the mental health field became the nightmare it had become. The Haynes' had moved to the Central Texas area several years back saying he would never do a full load of one on one counseling again. "This has got to be the part where you never say never," he had learned from prior experience. He sat down to catch his breath and ponder his next move. He was thrilled for his neighbors, the Wilson's, but he was likewise stunned at the prospect of having to work with a large number of substance abusers that would probably be mandated by the probation department to enter the program he'd developed. Right now, his school was very successful and he did nothing but train others to do the one on one work he had done for years. He was 62 and his life was slowing down a wee bit. He was doing what he was highly trained to do, but he still had time for a life that he finally had become fully contented with.

"God," he prayed putting his face in his hands. "Are you trying to disturb me at the point of my comfort? Is that what this is all about? You know that working with addicts is like working in the land of miss-fit toys." This is what Michael had always called that population of people. "What a world of pain and heartache. Is this really what you want me to do? I will have to say that it is obvious that You opened this door. I have never known a state agency to give an inmate to a faith-based counselor. Or any other counselor for that matter. This has got to be You. There is no other explanation!" His prayer was fervent.

He remembered all of the days he sat in his office and listened to people spew out the garbage of their lives and the messes they had made for themselves while all the time expecting him to fix them. "Yeah, right!" he thought. "I'm here for my weekly session, Dr. Haynes – fix me!" He sat on his patio for another hour looking at the Wilson's house across the alley and wondering what they were thinking. He knew that they were extremely worried, but he wanted to formulate some type of treatment plan before he told them the news. With pad in hand, he moved to his chase lounge and began to do what he was exceptionally good at doing. After a while of creative thought, he took a deep breath, told Marj where he was going, and moved into the alley headed for Bob and Ann's.

"Michael," Marj called out over the fence. "Take them a CD of Turn Your Eyes On Me." This was a recording she had made for the victims of the Ground Zero attack on September 11. She had written the title song years before.

"Great idea!" Michael said and returned to meet her in the driveway.

He moved between the houses and rang the Wilson's front door and rang the bell. It was almost instantly opened with both Bob and Ann standing there along with Tom's daughters and Nellie. He could tell they were on pins and needles about Tom, but he sensed something different in their demeanor. They were much more confident than when he left them earlier. At least that's what he felt it might have been.

"You guys have been reading, haven't you?" he asked.

"Ever since you left. We can't believe that we never knew what you do. You would have been seeing much more of us had we been aware," Ann said. "I've got a million questions, but tell us what they said."

"I'm going to tell you exactly what they told me. When I called, Tim said he had good news and bad news. He said that there was no way that Tom could get out of going to prison Substance Abuse Felony Punishment for 6 months." The girls started crying. Bob put his arm around Ann. "However, they gave him to me until it is time for him to go. In other words, he does not have to remain in county jail until the SAFP space is available which could be up to 12 or 15 weeks."

"Oh, thank God!" Ann slumped. Bob turned away so his tears wouldn't be visible. He shook his fist downward in a victory shake. Ann hugged her mom as if a temporary stay of execution had been granted.

"However, guys, I need to talk to you about how this absolutely must take place. Could we all sit down? Everyone, please," Michael said softly. They went into the den and everyone found a seat. He was not really comfortable with the setting, but there was no other option considering the situation.

"Let me once again be blatantly honest with you. Tom is in serious trouble. There are people going to prison in this area for lengthy sentences and much lesser offenses than Tom has against him. I will never tell you anything to unnecessarily frighten you or add to your hurt. So, please do not take offense at what I am about to say, but if we aren't on the same page I cannot and will not counsel Tom in any manner." Michael was gentle but ever so firm. "Can we agree?" he continued. Everyone nodded or answered affirmatively.

"For the better part of his life or probably all of his life, you guys have enabled Tom. Whatever he wanted, he got. Whenever he was in trouble, you bailed him out. Whenever he needed something, you gave it to him. There was never any visible responsibility or accountability that wasn't strictly about him and there has never been any consequence he has had to face for his actions. In essence, what you intended for good for your son has turned out to be the root of his near destruction."

The only silence that Bob and Ann could ever remember being more intense was the silence in the courtroom a couple of days before. Michael continued, "The probation department has done something to test me and the program I have produced for them. I will explain all of that later. But, really they are going to test us all. Truth be known, I don't have much to lose if we fail. The only one at serious risk here is Tom. We are embarking on uncharted turf with the State of Texas Criminal Justice System. If you in anyway shield Tom from accepting the responsibility for what he has done and the offenses he has incurred, it will be the worst thing that could possibly ever happen to him."

After a few brief moments, Bob and Ann spoke almost at the same time, "For the first time, we understand."

Then Bob said, "Dr. Haynes, we have been enabling each other for so long we might need your help to show us when we are doing it."

"I understand. And added to that, I received a mandate from my Lord Jesus Christ to help your family however I can. I may make some mistakes – we all may make some mistakes, but I have been spiritually convinced that if we work together, I believe in my heart that nothing but good things can come from all of the evil of the past." He waited to let that sink in. "Tom will be ready at 9:00 am or there about and you can pick him up then. Take him home and let him shower and change clothes. Bob, you stay with him even when he showers. Then, call me when he is ready and bring him to me. I will meet him on my patio, explain what is expected of him and we will go from there. Oh, and by the way, here is a CD that Marj produced with an original song entitled "Turn Your Eyes On Me" that she wrote in the mid 80's when she was going through some severe trials. It has deeply touched and ministered to the needs of countless numbers of hurting people who are experiencing burdens of all sorts."

Michael left. Ann went immediately to the CD player and started the song. As the powerful words came from Marj's equally powerful voice, Bob, Ann, Nellie wept and thanked God for His intervention. "Angels are among us," Nellie whispered.

She said those exact words to Marj during a conversation they had the very next day on the Haynes' patio as they prayed for Tom.

Chapter Four

"Tom, I'm not buying into what they want you to do," echoed Tom's savvy probation officer. I hope this Dr. Haynes guy knows his stuff and knows you. The decision for you to stay out of jail and start some counseling program with him came from our director, not me, so you better watch your butt, 'cause I'm sure going to," his PO continued. "I'm going to be around every corner and if you have the slightest hint of a dirty UA, or if you miss seeing me one time, its back to county. Understood?"

"Yep!" Tom took his usual posture swaying with his head bowed and only a brief, frequent, and impersonal glance toward thtose who were in authority over him. They knew his game but he knew it better. He had invented it. Making little innocent child like movements with his swaying as he moved his feet back and forth made him look like an innocent child who got caught with his hand in the cookie jar. That was how he became so non threatening and it usually disarmed everyone in situations like the one he was currently facing. The tactic had always worked – especially with his parents. If that game didn't work with Bob and Ann, he would just get mad and fight with them until they gave in or up. But now he knew that it was only a matter of hours until he could get into the surroundings that fit his addiction like a pair of expensive gloves. All he had to do was wait. Soon, he would be able to use some 'meth' and that feeling would flood what was left of his brain and drown his constant pain and the guilt that accompanied it.

Tom Wilson's life was a complete mess. A muddled mass of confusion and clutter. He had been told in no uncertain terms by his probation officer that he was not sold on the idea of him leaving county jail and being put in some faith based counseling program. His PO had heard of Dr. Haynes from his bosses and directors of community supervision, but had never met him. Consequently, as a seasoned probation officer he had serious doubts about his supervisors decision, but there was nothing he could do about it. Plus, he truly wanted Tom to get clean and turn his life around. He just wasn't convinced that this was the way that could happen.

Tom still couldn't believe that he'd gotten away with it one more time. Of course, he realized that prison was out there waiting for him somewhere sometime, but that would be a while off now and he only lived for the moment anyway, so that was OK with him. He already had his competition planned. How he was going to use this opportunity to play his games again. Only this time, he had been sent up to the big 'show.' He was now playing in the majors. He was toying with fire. Bring it on was his attitude. It was him against them and he wasn't going to lose this one! Dope was his strength to overcome anything and had become his best friend over the past few years. He had given up everything for its company and any one who stood in his way to hinder his reunion was his enemy.

The door slammed as the PO left and Tom was in the holding room alone. He had heard that clanging slam far too many times for him. "Patience," he thought. Waiting good-naturedly and staying cool was the order at hand. How long he'd have to wait, he didn't know. He looked around. All he saw was the typical environment of a cell. There was nothing but a bunk, a pot and a sink. At first he adjusted the rolled up mattress on the bunk to find his best comfort spot and then he just slumped back with his arm behind his head. He planed to doze away the time until his dad came to get him. Dad always came to get him.

He closed his eyes and immediately fell into a kind of twilight sleep – half in and half out of consciousness. Even though he didn't want it to happen, thoughts about his family began to creep down the corridors of his unprotected and relaxed mind. Normally he could manage to keep that kind of thinking blocked or repressed. But this time he couldn't. In came memories of his mom and dad, Kelly and his girls, Kelly's parents and how they had treated him in the past, his grandparents. There was an enormous amount of fiery darts that had all converged to the forefront of his reflection and unwanted tears began to swell. Tom was far from stupid or even ignorant. He knew what he had done to hurt the one's he loved most as well as what he had done to himself. He'd blown the partnership with his grand dad in the dairy because of his addiction and lost more money than he ever wanted to remember. He'd blown a normal relationship with his mom and dad. He's blown his relationship with his wife and girls. He's blown almost everything he could think of, but these were really what mattered most. And now, he was even considering blowing the last chance he may ever have to stay out of a long prison sentence.

As Tom lay there waiting he lost all track of time. He didn't know if he was dreaming or awake and aware, but whatever he was feeling was really weird. His life was passing before his very eyes. Sort of like what he had always heard about when a person is drowning. Was he drowning? He knew he wasn't drowning in water. Maybe the past and all of the mistakes he had made and the grief he had caused were flooding in making him think he was drowning. His chest grew heavy. Deep breaths came hard. He didn't know what was happening, but he couldn't stop the overflow of the past from catching up and forcing its way in. He had hidden these thoughts for years. He had tried to cover up and mask what he didn't want to deal with or let himself feel by using dope or whatever he could find to take his mind far away from where he really was. Thus far, he had been successful. But at this point in time, in this holding cell as he waited, there was nothing he could do to make them go away and they were overcoming him.

He had been off the drugs long enough for his mind to have somewhat of a degree of focus. "OK," he whispered, "I'll let it go and get it over with," he thought. "Let's get this picture in order." It was like he was in the shoot on a bucking bull with his hand in the harness saying to the gatekeepers, "Turn him loose!" And the gate opened. God only knew what would be the outcome of allowing himself to think about the past. He sure didn't.

He entered his mental time machine and it took him all the way back to those early bull riding days. He remembered drinking, fighting and partying, but his main goal of a rodeo career was what his mind focused on because at that time that was the only thing he wanted. He wanted a career in rodeo and nothing could stop him or get in his way. He got what he wanted and became a very successful cowboy, but was it his obsessive-compulsive behavior patterns that had caused him to go from the early days of triumph and achievement and fun to where he was now? As he deeply considered it, he admitted he had dropped everything to ride bulls. He continually did whatever it took to follow what he wanted to do in that arena. It was always all about him. It always had been all about him.

Tom was on the professional rodeo circuit for nine years. He was in the top thirty cowboys every year, but that didn't pay much. So, Bob and Ann helped him financially all of those years and he got used to it. Tom had married his rookie year, but he did good to be at home one weekend every three months. During the times he was at home he fathered two children. Two children and a wife he really didn't know and who really didn't know him because he was never there.

Tom, Kelly, Kayla, and London   Tom and London

He couldn't believe he had missed the little things that a father watches as his kids grow up, but he did. Everything had always been given to Tom on a silver platter so that he could further his career and he took advantage of everything and everyone he could. His goal was to be a world champion no matter what the cost. "Oh God," he thought as his eyes teared up. "I can never get any of that back. It's just gone. Time, money, businesses, relationships – gone."

"And, my little sister, Trisa," Tom sobbed to himself and buried his head. She always loved me not matter what. She really got the brunt of my stupidity."

Tom and Trisa while Tom Is on Rodeo Circuit

Tom's journey through his past received a welcomed interruption by the clanging of a metal door at the other end of the hall. "All Right!" he thought. "Finally! Dad's here to get me out of this garbage dump. What the hell took him so long?" He waited anxiously to see Bob round the corner. "I'll be floating high tonight," he imagined finally getting a deep breath. But when the jail guard rounded the corner, his expectations sunk. "Crap," he thought looking at the uniformed officer with obvious contempt.

"Hey Wilson," scoffed the officer. "I hear you've got some rich old man who has pulled some strings," he muttered with sarcasm. He was trying to get a rise out of Tom so they could find someway to keep him where they thought he belonged.

"Nah," responded Tom in a pseudo polite manner. He was determined to be very careful not to let the guard see his real expression. He didn't want anything to confuse the issue of him getting out.

"Well, ain't nobody come for yuh yet," he smirked. "If they don't come soon, guess we've got your sorry ass for a 'nuther night, huh? He paused looking straight into Tom's eyes. And, who knows what can happen in a night?" He laughed, as he turned and walked off still cackling banging the bars with his stick.

"Where'd they find these guys," Tom thought and lay back down on the bunk. He was glad for the break, however. His past had become much too intrusive for him to enjoy reliving it. But, the reflections picked up immediately and uncontrollably, and like before, there was nothing he could do but let them come again.

Tom Wilson's dairy farm and cattle

His mind went back to his failed dairy business, the loss of over a million dollars, his and his family's inheritance, and it was all because of his drug use.

Tom remembered how that when he was high all of his plans for successful ventures seemed to be right. When he was on the drug, he felt he could conquer everything and achieve anything. He believed his ideas so convincingly that his dad and granddad always went along with his hyped up plans even though they knew there was a very high risk of failure. To Tom's drug crazed mind, everything made perfect sense. To Bob and Royce, nothing made sense and they never really knew how much their enabling was leading to Tom's downfall.

Tom painfully remembered talking his dad and granddad out of so much money the guilt he felt about that became almost too overwhelming for him to bear. Of course, they had let him do what he had done, but were It not for him, they never would have entered his nonsensical schemes. He hated remembering it, but now that he had been drug free long enough for him to think straight, he was getting a clear picture of the carnage he had left behind while he was in his addiction. "God how could I have done this to the ones I love the most?" he repeated once more. "My grandparents of all things?"

Royce and Nellie Meadows, Tom's grandparents and Ann's mom and dad

Tom thought about the arguments he had purposefully caused with his mom and dad for the sole motivation of isolating himself. People in deep addiction always tend to isolate themselves from their families. Probably for the simple reason they don't want to be seen in the true state they are in. Tom's addiction was so serious he was using $3,000 to $4,000 dollars of methamphetamine on a weekly basis. His memories were really kind of a blur, but he was able to think back to the time he had to start selling drugs because it was the only way he could support an addiction of his size.

Tom snickered and cried at the same time when he thought of how Bob and Ann had even helped him to get a place right down the street from where they lived. He wanted to be close to the source, but never shouldered an ounce of responsibility. He never paid any bills. No matter how much money he was making, he used his money to play not pay. Bob and Ann paid the bills. And, even though Tom was physically close to his parents, he didn't see them but about once every couple of months. Whenever he saw his kids walking down the street, he would hide or play possum and act asleep.

Tom's addiction escalated to the degree that even selling the drug didn't take care of what his needs were. Even with all of his use and the chaos that surrounded him, it never entered his mind that he might get caught and sent to prison.

At the same time that God began to deal with Ann about the fact that something was critically wrong with her son, Tom was on his 10th dirty urine analysis and he was still on probation. He thought about that and had to conclude that only God could have kept him out of a lengthy prison sentence. "Only God," he whispered. "Three dirty UA's and I could have easily gotten a 15 years." As he was reliving all of the horror of the past 8 years, he could see much more clearly that there was something unusually spiritual going on. He had never really been against God in his heart, but his mind had been entirely captured by the demons in methamphetamine. He recalled how his dad was always trying to talk to him about the Lord and the fact that he should be a better father and get his family back in church. But, connected to that memory were the constant heated squabbles they would get into because he just didn't want to hear it.

He manipulated all of his probation officers and could always talk them into giving him another chance. Anyone else would have long since been serving time. Then he reflected on the one probation officer he ran into that he couldn't fool. It was for sure she was going to revoke his probation. She said she would give him 60 days at a local rehab center and if he succeeded, she would take that into consideration. But, under no uncertain terms, if he had another dirty UA, he was off to prison.

The deal she made with the judge and Tom was that Tom had to be clean to enter the rehab and if he showed up unclean he would immediately receive a 10-year prison term. There would be no discussion and no other option. Tom had three days to get clean and enter the program or the Texas Department of Criminal Justice would be his new home for 10 years without chance for parole.

Somehow he remained clean for the three days and was admitted to the program, which Bob was going to pay $30,000 for him to enter. Tom instantaneously began not only to use drugs in the rehab, but he was smooth enough to market the stuff on the very premises. He even had people meeting him in the woods to bring him drugs for his own use and to sell to anyone else in the program who wanted to grab a high.

As Tom lay there sprawled on the bunk in that holding cell, he vividly remembered that a savvy counselor had given him a random urine check and he knew he would turn up dirty which meant he would be kicked out of the program and be sent to prison. The only thing that was on his warped mind at that time was the fact that he needed to escape. He just knew he could do what he had always done and clear out. Disappear. In his cloudy messed up thinking he still believed that he could simply leave and get completely away from the system and still do what he wanted to do. Tom was the master game player – the best. But his final game had been played and there was nothing else left to do but run. Without the slightest delay he turned his back on the rehab center, jumped the fence and ran as far as he could as fast as he could without a clue what to do or where to go. He left everything there and was wearing nothing but his shorts.

This rehabilitation center was miles in the country, so he remembered he had to run through deep cedar infested brush in miles of barren land and would finally wind up in the middle of nowhere. He thought to himself, "How stupid! What did I think I was going to do?" he thought when he finally stopped. Tom had not slept for two days and when he stopped he recalled just lying down in a dry riverbed under some cedar brush with his face in the dirt. His addiction was so strong that he had to do dope just to stay awake. If he ever got still, he'd just pass out. And, that's exactly what happened. He went to sleep in that riverbed completely vulnerable to all of the critters and insects that made their home in that field.

He didn't know how long he lay there, but when he came too he was covered with ant bites and scratches. His paranoid mind told him that they would be sending dogs after him like he was an escaped felon. This rehab center was close to Fort Hood, and Tom heard helicopters hovering overhead on maneuvers, but he thought they were looking for him. He didn't move a muscle even though insects, spiders and the cedar brush that he had covered himself with were devouring him.

All of a sudden, as he lay under that brush in the dirt he heard his name being called. "Tommy! Tommy! Where are you? Come on back and we'll work things out." Tom thought he was dreaming until he peered out from under the brush and saw his dad's shoes not three feet from him. It was all he could do not to respond and come out. His heart was pounding out of his chest and the tears literally streamed down his dust caked face. But he knew that his dad would take him back to the treatment center, so he kept still and quite as hard as it was.

As Tom was lying on his bunk waiting to be released, he could not escape the pain of thinking back about that moment in time when he reached the bottom of his brokenness. In his mind he the words kept getting louder, "Tommy! Tommy! Please come out!" his dad kept calling. Tom remembered he could tell that his dad was crying by his broken voice. He was crying for his son trying desperately to save his life and Tom was close enough to actually reach out and touch his dad's foot. Back in that ditch, after what seemed like an eternity, Bob finally got in his car and moved on slowly down the road still yelling for Tommy.

"God!" Tom whispered a prayer of desperation. He kept his head down in the red dust that covered his face every time he took a breath. "How did it come to this? I don't know what to do? I'm sorry for not being what I should have been. I love my kids. I love my mom and dad. How could I have gotten things so twisted and out of wack? God, my grandparents. Oh God! What have I done – what have I done to them? What am I going to do now?" he silently continued to weep. He knew if someone heard him he would be in for some wicked abuse, so he stayed in still and quiet with ants and spiders still crawling all over his scratched and sunburned body. "God, please help me," he cried out under his breath. "I don't know which way to turn."

It was in that old dry riverbed that something began to happen in Tom Wilson's spirit. He was looking up to see bottom and he realized for the first time that he had brought it all on himself. There was no one to blame but him. When he finally owned up to that and cried out to God, it was a definite turning point in his life.

In the cell that night while he was waiting, every stupid and evil thing he had ever done was bearing down on him and crushing his inner self. If he could have stood up and screamed to the top of his lungs he would have. If he could have beaten himself to a pulp he would have. But he knew if he did anything to call attention to himself, they wouldn't let him go. He had never experienced such an emotional upheaval. He had never let himself. He was fun loving Tom – the life of the party. But in those few moments that seemed like time had literally stopped, Tom Wilson came face to face with Tom Wilson and he didn't at all like what he saw. In a word, he was being broken like a matchstick in a hurricane. God was bringing about the work of inner conviction that only He can do. There was no way that Tom could reconcile, explain or escape what was happening inside him. It was like all of the wars that had ever happened on the planet were taking place in his mind. There was an incredible battle being waged for his soul. What he was feeling was far beyond confusion. He couldn't come up with a description that was even close to where his emotions were taking him. For the first time he could ever think of, he felt like he was falling beyond his control into some huge black hole. "Oh God!" he shivered. "Please please help me! I'm going crazy! Help me!"

It was at the height – the peak of his anguish that he heard the main door at the end of the hall making that same loud clanking sound again. He was hurting so bad it took him by surprise and he almost didn't hear it. He quickly turned over so no one could see his expression if it happened to be that same guard again. As he wiped his nose and face with his sleeve and slowly turned back over and peeked. When he did, he found himself staring straight into the face of his dad. The shock almost set his soul on fire. Even then, he was at a total loss as to what his sentiments should be. He tried to appear in control, but he knew that Bob instantly pierced his defense shields and saw everything he had been hiding for years behind his eyes. In that moment, his dad connected to the true heart of his son. In that split second of eye contact, Tom was acutely aware that his dad knew everything about the reality of all of his lies, the stealing, the cheating, the game playing, the hustling. He knew he knew. Everything was laid emotionally bare and for the first time in ages they both were finally on the same page.

After Tom and Bob signed all of the paper work and walked out the front door of the jail, Ann was standing by the car waiting. She was crying and didn't care who was watching. The deputies and other inmates were walking by and neither she, Bob or Tom cared what anyone might think about them gathering in a circle of three and holding each other. This was their son – their prodigal son who had just returned home. Gods grace had brought him out of bondage he could have never conquered on his own. They didn't know at the time, but Tom's offenses were really much worse than most of the other guys that passed them dressed in orange. Nevertheless, the past went out the window. He was in their arms and for the moment it was like heaven had moved into earth on their behalf and had lifted all of them out of a dismal miry pit.

After a moment, they got into the car and left as quickly as they could. No one said anything. Finally, not knowing how Tom would react, Bob told him that Dr. Haynes' wife Marj had written a song and he and Ann wanted him to listen to it on the way home. Tom didn't argue. They put the CD in the player and the music and words began to fill the air as if they were coming from heaven itself. *"Turn your eyes on me, I can feel your pain. I know the hurt you feel my child, but you're not alone; I'm here to stay – right by your side, to see you through. Turn your eyes on me, I'll always be with you."*

Tom could not control his feelings or hold them back. He didn't even try. He openly began to cry as he listened to the words of the song. It was then that Bob and Ann Wilson knew for sure in their heart of hearts that they had finally gotten their son back. It had been a long way home.

You Can Run, But You Can't Hide
Chapter Five

Bob Wilson had surrendered for the gospel ministry at the age of 14 at a summer youth camp with his church. He was now 61. Over the course of his life he had been personally involved in well over 30 business ventures or start-ups and that is a conservative estimate. He was successful at most everything he tried. However, there had always been a void – an inner emptiness continued to plague him when he reached his goals in these various endeavors, and he had never really been able to put a finger on why. In the deepest recesses of his heart he probably knew what was wrong, but he had become so distracted and seared over through the years with so many new and different challenges, it never really dawned on him until now that he had been running from his calling for most of his life.

One of the key turning points for Bob was when he, Ann and Nellie went to New Orleans just to get away and catch a change of pace before Tom was to be incarcerated in the SAFP program. One evening they were walking down a street in the French Quarter and saw a clean-cut young man sitting in the darkened corner of a doorway holding out a tin cup and asking for money. Before all of the things that had happened with his son, Bob would have walked on past the young man and thought, "Get up and get a job. What's wrong with you? You're nothing but a bum and a drain on taxpayers!" But his spirit was instantly convicted and he was vividly reminded that the boy could have just as easily been Tommy sitting there had he not of been provided with family means to enable his addiction. And for sure, this kid was somebody's son.

After walking on by, Bob couldn't get the young man off of his mind. He shared his feelings with Ann and she told him that the same thing had happened in her heart. Right then and there, the Wilson's decided to make it their life goal to help addicts and their families who were in bondage to the devastating effects of substance abuse. On that trip they determined to fight the dragon with every weapon they could find.

Major changes were taking place in the Wilson's lives. Spiritual changes. During the time that Dr. Haynes was counseling and working with Tom, Bob and Ann were asking every question they could think of and learning all they could about chemical dependency and the dynamics of addiction. This went on for several weeks prior to Tom being sent to the Substance Abuse Felony Punishment unit in North Texas, which was about a 3-hour drive from home.

Substance Abuse Felony Punishment Unit at Breckinridge, TX

The program was to last 6 months. He was allowed two visitors for two hours every Saturday and Bob and Ann were always there. Sometimes Tom's girls, his grandmother Nellie, and his girlfriend Angie made the trip to visit. But most of the time it was just Bob and Ann. They wanted to see the end results of someone being sent to prison because of drug abuse. They were eager to know how they had contributed to Tom's problems and what they could have done to stop it so they could tell their story to other parents who found themselves in the same situation. Bob, especially, was looking for clues as to what had happened to cause Tom's addiction and why they had not seen the underlying disorder for far too many years. It was so clear to them now and truly befuddled them how they had either been blind or purposefully overlooked the obvious signs and symptoms of the abuse by the bizarre behavior it causes. Especially since Tommy had always been so close to them. Could it have been they just didn't want to see it or admit it? Maybe they knew deep down what the problem might be and were simply embarrassed for anyone else to know. Or were they totally clueless as to what they were dealing with. Whatever the case was, they were both in absolute agreement that this was where God wanted them to begin their life core ministry. They had been praying for a long time that God would show them what He wanted them to do rather than just sit on a pew Sunday after Sunday. They knew in their hearts that they wanted to go further and do more to help advance the Kingdom. They just didn't know what or where or how to start. Now, they were assured that this was it, so they began to apply themselves and take advantage of all of the training they could find. The drug world had never been a part of their world, so they had to come very close to entering the gates of hell itself to learn how to minister to addicts.

First, the Wilson's enrolled in the Faith Based Counselor Training Institute, and took the Basic and Advanced courses on the Spiritual Dynamics of Addiction, Anger Management, and others. They had received their state recognized certification as Restorative Therapists™, Anger Management Specialists™ and Personality Profile Consultants. They had bought and read every book they could get their hands on that concerned the sweeping drug problem in the country. However, they noticed as they searched for material that there wasn't really very much in print that addressed what parents should do when they finally discover their children's drug abuse. They were blown away when they discovered that America is 6% of the world's population and Americans consumed 68% of the world's illicit drugs. Not only that, they learned that prescription medication killed more people in one year than all of the wars the nation had ever faced. They had completely immersed themselves into becoming aware of what the drug culture was really like without being alert as to where this all of their work and study was taking them in their overall life purpose.

Bob and Ann Group Counseling

Dr. Haynes had allowed them to begin to counsel and work with addicts who were on probation and parole through his treatment center and under his supervision. He had sat in on the sessions and mentored them during the hands on training process. He had allowed them to take leadership roles in the groups and had introduced them to Alcoholics Anonymous and Narcotics Anonymous and the principles behind those programs. He taught them how to spot the games that some people play and how to tell if people were really serious about their recovery. As it ended up, they were really working almost full time with addicts and people who had anger problems. He had used them to teach a block of curriculum for the Faith Based Counselor Training schools.

Bob and Ann Wilson teach Personality Profiles In FBCTI school

One afternoon as they were leaving the clinic, Michael said, "Bob, you know what you and Ann are really doing is full time ministry." He said it in passing not knowing that Bob had surrendered his life to full time ministry when he was a teenager. Michael might as well have dropped a ton of bricks on Bob's head through his words. It all hit home with that simple statement. Bob thought about it on his drive home. "Ann, what we are really doing is full time ministry. For the first time since I was fourteen years old I believe I have finally begun to fulfill my calling."

"Wow!" Ann said softly. "I guess you are right. We are working with the same kind of sick people that Jesus worked with."

On that note, nothing else was said until they entered their driveway and garage. Bob immediately went to his office to think about how they had gradually grown into a full-blown ministry. "I need to talk to Pastor Jeff about this," he whispered. "God, is this the real thing? It's nothing like I thought of back at that summer youth camp so many years ago. Am I finally doing what you called me to do?"

There were so many questions that both he and Ann had about the things they were experiencing on a day-by-day basis. This was certainly nothing like anything they had ever done. It was a completely different and new world for them and they were spending every waking hour getting educated about everything they could so they could be more effective in helping those who were trapped in the throngs of addiction. It had become their only true passion. The more they counseled with those affected by the problem, the more they gradually learned that some people really wanted out of their addiction and have their lives changed, but didn't know how to find true freedom. While on the other hand, some only said they wanted out but they really weren't ready to 'own their stuff' and take responsibility for their negative consequence behavior and the souls they had crushed and lives they had ruined in the wake of their cravings. Bob and Ann were finally becoming somewhat skilled at being able to separate the sheep from the goats, so to speak.

The following weekend they made the three-hour drive the night before their two-hour visit on Saturday. The unit where Tom was incarcerated was a small town with no nice hotel or motel to stay, but they would have had to get up in the wee hours of the morning to make it to the prison on time for the visit, so they spent the night in the only dump available.

"How are you Tommy," Bob and Ann asked after going through the lengthy and demeaning process it takes to visit with any inmate locked up in the Texas Department of Criminal Justice.

"Dad, this is hell in here!" moaned Tom. "I was leaning up against my window last week watching a deer move through the woods outside. A guard saw me and made me wash all of the stupid baseboards in the unit with a toothbrush. Even the latrine! Damn! It took nine hours and I still didn't finish. I could barely stand up. I didn't do anything to deserve that."

Tom went on and on about what was going on inside the unit. Unless someone had been an inmate, they would be totally clueless about the kind of pandemonium and chaos he was trying to describe. Ann had written Tom and asked him if he could give them copies of the programs they were using. He said he couldn't get that for them but they could ask the lady they had been talking to whose son had being released that day to give them his. She did. The two hours seemed like ten minutes and then they were told to leave as the guards came and got Tom. They barely had a chance to say goodbye.

On the way home, Ann began to look through some of the material her friend had given them. "Bob, listen to this," she finally said. The title of this lesson is Stages To Chemical Dependency." She began to read out loud. After all, they had a long way to go so there was plenty of time to review the material. Maybe there was something they could use in their newfound ministry.

Stages of Substance Abuse

The use of a substance for mood alteration constitutes substance abuse. Dependence substance usually occurs over a period of time, and follows a pattern. Treatment providers have determined that the earlier the detection occurs the greater the chances for recovery are, and they have identified four basic stages relevant to the abuse of chemicals.

Stage 1 —Experimentation

The use of substances out of boredom or for recreational purposes may lead to dependence. Use at this stage may not result in negative consequences and may be difficult to detect. A child may, however, be establishing a lifelong pattern. Too many youngsters and adults believe that the first use of alcohol and other drugs is safe. For youths, using drugs as tobacco and alcohol is often, unfortunately, viewed as normal. However, because young bodies are particularly susceptible to alcohol and other drugs and their effects, there is no such thing as totally "safe" use of any mind altering-drug by a youngster. In stage one, however, there may be no outward behavioral changes caused by the use of drugs. Still, such experimentation should not be tolerated.

104

Stage 2 — More Regular Use

The second stage involves more frequent use of alcohol or other drugs as the person actively seeks the euphoric effects of a mind-altering drug. At this point, the user establishes a reliable source, and may add mid-week use of alcohol or other drugs to previous habits of weekend use at parties. Behavioral changes, lying, deterioration of friends and planning of times to use mark this stage. Intervention at this point is imperative in order to avoid allowing the child to slip into dependency. Significant to this step is not the amount or frequency of use as much as its effect on the user.

Stage 3 — Daily Preoccupation

In stage three, there is intense preoccupation with the desire to experience euphoric effects. Living will begin to center around drug availability and use. Problems with parents, police, and friends will begin to increase. More and more time, energy, and money will be devoted to abuse. The user may feel they can quit at any time, but it is evident that they choose not to.

Stage 4 — Dependency

In the fourth stage, increasing levels are needed just to feel OK. Physical signs such as coughing, frequent sore throats, weight loss *and fatigue —, which may have begun to appear earlier, — are now common. Being high becomes normal. Blackouts and overdosing also are more common, family life is a disaster, and crime may be becoming a way of life to obtain money to buy drugs. Delusion about the negative impact or destruction occurring causes continued **and** increased abuse.*

"I just can't comprehend why anyone would even want to do drugs, let alone like them," Ann said.

"Lets give it a break," Bob said after a while. "Are you hungry?"

"I could eat," she said after closing the folder. "You know, it only takes common sense to spot these symptoms. If parents could just be attentive and spot the beginning stages they might be able to spare themselves the humiliation of seeing their child in the circumstances we just left."

Both of them were a little depressed and embarrassed that there was nothing they could do for Tom. He was out of their hands and out of their ability to rectify the life changing mistakes he had made. In other words, for a time he was beyond their enabling reach.

They felt a little better after eating, but didn't open the folder anymore during the drive. Finally, late in the afternoon of their first visit, they were home. They had this same pattern to look forward to every weekend for six long months. They were both dead tired. Ann called her mom, which was a long time custom, and gave her a rundown of the visit detail for detail. They decided they would call the others in the morning and they went to bed and to sleep without much more conversation.

Bob turned over. It was barely light outside and it was Sunday. Ann was not in the bed. "Ann," he called.

"I'm in here reading," she responded. He turned back over and closed his eyes. All he could see was Tom in handcuffs. He wrestled with the images for a few minutes and then rolled out.

After a while he came out to the room they had glassed in to make it look like they were outside. "Are you still looking through that folder," he asked. He didn't really want to get into a discussion right then because they were almost late for church.

"We need to get ready, and I need to look over my lesson," Bob yawned. He taught an adult Sunday School class at his church and had it in his mind to tell them all about their situation. They went through the standard Sunday-get-ready routine, but there was something different about today. "Ann, don't be embarrassed, but I'm going to tell our class about our visit yesterday."

"It's OK, Bob. We need their prayers. Tell them everything. You said we needed to get into the fight."

Bob and Ann were elated that they had finally been able to unburden years of pent up feelings, and their friends had nothing but supportive things to say.

"I should have done that months ago," Bob said as they were walking from the class to church.

"I know," Ann responded. "Now, we can get on about our ministry and have the prayer support of others. That was a good thing to do."

When the sermon was over, Bob, Ann, and Nellie went out to eat and then immediately home. Ann had remembered during church that Dr. Haynes had given them some material on one of his first visits that he had written years ago entitled Ten Steps to Take When You Discover Your Child is On Drugs. She shuffled through the mounds of papers and books, and finally found the little article.

"If we are going to organize ourselves to be able to tell other parents about things they can do when they find out their children have a drug problem. Maybe we can build our program on these ten steps that Michael brought over earlier," Ann mentioned to Bob as she sat down at her computer. "Lets talk about these and see how they fit our own story."

Ten Steps to Take When You Discover Your Child is On Drugs
By Dr. Michael K. Haynes

Step One: Overcoming Denial; Admitting the problem; Dealing with embarrassment

These were subtitles in each step.

"I believe the first step is the hardest thing I have ever had to do," said Bob. "It might be as hard or harder for other parents. We just didn't want anyone to know once we found out ourselves."

"Yes, but look how long it took us to find out what was really happening," replied Ann. "We were in a major state of denial. How do we get people to see that they might be in denial about their own family secrets?"

"I don't know, but that is the step that must be dealt with first," answered Bob. "Like I've said before, the devil slips in the back door and hides out for a while, then all of a sudden he is right in your face. When that truly happens, denial goes out the window."

"I agree," said Ann.

Step Two: Locate good counselors; must take faith based approach; get to the root of addiction; drugs are only a symptom.

We didn't know any counselors at all," admitted Ann. "Let alone good counselors who knew about addiction and how to work with people who had the problem."

"Maybe we need to ask Michael who some of the better counselors in the area are and maybe we should set up a network so that we can refer people when they need help," Bob said. "You know people are going to ask."

"Great thought!" Ann agreed. "Let me start a list of things we need to do."

Step Three: Do not fear entering the land of 'miss-fit toys;' greater is He that is in you than he that is in the world; read and study the dynamics of addiction; find a place to do hands on work as a volunteer; learn how addicts think.

"Man, we are fortunate to have been able to be trained and certified and have had some experience so that we can counsel these people and learn how they do think." Bob said.

"I would have never known how to do hands on work with even my own son had we not had the opportunity we have now. This has got to be a 'God thing,'" Ann agreed again.

Step Four: Learn to recognize the signs and symptoms of drug abuse; learn the games addicts play; know when manipulation is happening; know when someone is lying; become observant; learn to mix love and justice (velvet and steel) when dealing with addicts; people who abuse drugs will not stay around shame, so do not be shame based in your counseling; addicts already have enough personal shame without anyone else adding to it.

"Brother, am I ever guilty of that!" whispered Bob. "I tried to shame Tommy into doing right nearly all of the time. No wonder we constantly got into arguments. That's probably why he just seemed to tune me out."

"Me too," said Ann. "I did the same thing." Tears began to swell.

Step Five: Realize there is no real justice in this life; understand that drugs are the scourge of the system; understand the

competition between users and cops; see the system as a tool for shaping and molding character for the good; get better not bitter

"I know personally that people need to hear the get better and not bitter part," said Ann.

"Uh huh," mumbled Bob. "For sure! I could really be bitter over this if I think about it too much," he admitted. "Just looking back at the money we lost would be enough to make most people bitter."

Step Six: Learn the power of accountability; owning your stuff; the necessity of consequences; tough love principles and action; the importance of boundaries and structure.

"It embarrasses me to death to think how far we missed this step. We didn't even know what tough love was, much less how to do it!" Bob and Ann both decided. The only thing they could do now is to tell others how they had failed in this area. They had been classic enablers, certainly not tough lovers.

Step Seven: Know what is required for recovery; the medical model; the failure of the established treatment industry; the steps to relapse; what causes relapse; the fight of all fights; switching addictions.

"I just can't say it enough. Little did we know at the time how much we would learn by going through FBCTI. I am so glad we did that and got our certification. Now, what is being said here, we halfway understand. We just need to develop our own testimony and get in front of as many people as we can," said Ann.

Step Eight: How to communicate with your kids about drugs; steps to proper intervention; taking action; get help; appeal to conscience.

"Most of this material is in The Drug Free Family PAK™," said Bob. We need to get that material out and go through it with a fine tooth comb."

"Then," responded Ann, "We need to try it out on some of our own clients to see if they would have listened to who ever was trying to help them."

Step Nine: Steps to prevention; instruction prior to use; understanding your kids world; know your kids friends and their parents; grant freedom when responsibility is demonstrated; balance freedom and responsibility; proper parenting principles

"We keep saying we've learned a lot, but we've sure got a lot more to learn," sighed Ann.

"Yep, but what else do we have to do that is more worthwhile," Bob immediately responded. *"I'm ready to go! I've run from my calling for too long. This is our ministry, I'm sure of it! This is exactly where God wants us."*

Step Ten: The testimony of an enabler; what enablers do; what happens when enablers don't stop enabling.

"This one won't be hard to write about," said Ann.

"You know Ann, as I look back on that youth camp and where we are today, its so clear just how great God has been to me – to us. I ran away from that calling for so long I forgot all about ever even saying those things or surrendering my life."

"I'm just glad He didn't forget," replied Ann with a slight smirk. "You know Bob, you can always run from Him, but you can never hide." Bob just looked at her and smiled.

How To Talk To Your Kids About Drugs

Chapter Six

"Bob," Ann was beginning her day with her usual cup of coffee. "We talked about shame yesterday. Remember?"

"I do," Bob responded. "What about it?"

"I thought about that a lot last night and wondered why we never really knew how to talk to Tom without trying to shame him to do what we thought he should be doing," she said reflectively. "What if we had really known how to confront him without him blowing sky high?"

"I don't know, but we definitely need to learn how to give other parents some solutions instead of just telling them our mistakes."

"I remember you saying that some of that material was in the Drug Free Family PAK™ that Michael left us."

"I think I remember seeing a video or a book," said Bob. "Let me go out to the garage and bring it in. Let's find out what all is in this thing."

Bob and Ann pulled out all of the tapes and books in the huge pack of information and began to look though it. "Here it is," exclaimed Bob. "It's a booklet on Intervention."

"Here is the video," said Ann. "Let's watch while we finish our coffee."

They popped the VCR in and listened to the same wonderful moderator they had heard a couple of times before.

"Intervention," boomed the big voice. Drug abuse can strike any family. Being aware of the early signs of abuse and knowing how to intervene quickly and properly are vitally important. This booklet and tape are designed to assist you in detecting and dealing with possible drug use in your family. Some of the areas we will discuss on this tape will include: Understanding the Progressive Stages of Substance Abuse; Recognizing the Signs and Symptoms of Substance Abuse; Detecting Alcohol and Other Drug Abuse; and Chemical Dependency A Family Problem

Let's ask ourselves a leading question, is my child using drugs?

Knowing for certain whether your child is or is not using drugs can be difficult for parents. Always begin by trusting your child, but do not blind yourself to the possible painful reality that your child is involved in substance abuse. There are common signs of drug use, but they are not usually obvious until use is occurring at a frequency of three times a week or more, and usually not until it has continued at that level for six months to two years.

Parenting is not the only influence on a child's development. One of the difficult lessons of parenting is learning to accept the difference between influence and control. Although we can be a powerful influence in the lives of our children and teenagers or even grown children, the actual controls are in their hands. For this reason, even responsible and capable parents can have a teenager who chooses to become involved with alcohol or other drugs. Effective parenting skills decrease the likelihood of this happening, but cannot absolutely prevent it.

As with any other problem that life poses, how we handle a teen's involvement will influence whether the problem is solved or worsens. Responsible parents must equip themselves to be able to detect violations of the family "no-use" rule and develop a firm and caring method of confronting their teenager's possible violation.

"This is going to be extremely important stuff," said Bob. "We may actually be able to help parents deal with this problem while their kids are still at home. If we can do that, I will be a happy camper. Tommy was already out of the nest, so we really didn't have much control or knowledge of what he was up to."

"Besides," agreed Ann, "he was never around. He was always gone."

The moderator continued. Parents absolutely must get Involved in Prevention and Detection. For any rule to be effective, you must be willing to expend the energy to detect violations. This includes the following:

- *imposing curfews*

- *knowing where your children are*

- *staying awake until your children come home at night and observing their behavior*

- *remaining informed and current in your knowledge of specific drugs (including alcohol) and their signs of use*

In addition, a concerned parent will:

• *learn about the extent of the alcohol and other drug problem in your community and schools;*

• *meet with parents of your children's friends or classmates*

• *establish a means with other parents of letting each other know which children are using alcohol and other drugs and who is supplying them*

• *become familiar with the common signs of abuse and share that awareness with your children*

Also, added to these practical things, parents should develop a real and meaningful spiritual relationship with their children; they should tell them about God; they should be a role model that the kid can learn from and mimic – 80% of all behavior is modeled behavior; they should always and consistently stand as a family support unit no matter what; they should always address the behavior and not the child when correction is necessary.

"There are certain Behavioral Characteristics Associated with Substance Abuse", he continued.

• *Abrupt changes in work or school attendance, quality of work, work output, grades, and discipline*

• *General attitude changes and/or irritability*

• *Withdrawal from responsibility*

• *Deterioration of physical appearance and grooming*

• *Impaired performance on the job or in the classroom*

• *Wearing of sunglasses at inappropriate times (to hide dilated or constricted pupils)*

• *Continual wearing of long-sleeved garments (to hide injection marks), particularly in hot weather, or reluctance to wear short-sleeved attire when appropriate*

• *Association with known substance abusers*

• *Unusual borrowing of money from friends, Co-workers, or parents*

• *Stealing small items from employer, home, or school*

• *Secretive behavior regarding actions and possessions; poorly concealed attempts to avoid attention and suspicion such as frequent trips to storage rooms, closets, restrooms, basements (to use drugs)*

Watch the eyes! The moderator emphasized.

When erratic behavior signs cause concern, look at the eyes. Abnormal eye signs may indicate either substance use or a medical or genetic condition which may be impairing the individual affected.

Drugs cause changes in behavior because they impact the brain. The ophthalmic system (which controls the eyes) is one of the first systems to be impacted by a chemical change in the body. Since proper eye function requires the extremely precise coordination of very small nerves and muscles, even small dosages of some drugs may disturb normal physiologic process and produce physical signs. The individual cannot override these changes by will. Therefore, changes in the function of the eye are an indicator of possible substance abuse.

When an individual's behavior becomes erratic, look into their eyes for these occurrences which may be signs of impairment:

Redness, excessive watering, and swelling of the eyelid

Heavy redness of the white of the eye which is not mere "contact scratch" or allergy lines will commonly occur with drunkenness or marijuana abuse.

Droopy eyelid

The eyelid does not normally rest on the pupil (black center) of the eye. Marijuana impacts the brain in such a way as to consistently cause this condition.

Retracted eyelid

This is referred to as "whitewall" or being "wide-eyed." The white of the eye is visible all the way around the colored area (iris) of the eye. This condition is usually apparent under the influence of some hallucinogens and amphetamines.

Pupil Dilation

In normal room light, the pupil will be about the same size as one third of the iris (colored portion) and will react to changes in light. A pupil which will not constrict in response to direct light stimulus is abnormal. A greatly enlarged pupil in average to bright light is also abnormal. This is a common brain response to marijuana. A very small pupil (pin-point) which seems fixed and non responsive is a strong indicator of opiate (heroin) use.

Rapid eye movement

Rapid side-to-side movement of the eye without the ability to fix for any period of time on an object is a sign of possible abuse of amphetamines or cocaine. The individual, who under normal conditions is able to look at you when being spoken to, seems unable to do so.

Impaired Tracking

A normal tracking of the eye across the iris will be smooth and non-impaired. Under the influence of certain chemicals, the eye will not be able to move without bouncing.

Non-Convergence

A normal eye should be able to cross and hold the crossed position for two to three seconds. An impaired condition exists when the eye cannot hold the crossed position for that period of time, but instead floats back to the center of the eye.

Why share eye signs with your child? Asked the speaker.

♦ *To help children RESIST the peer pressure to use drugs. Children whose parents recognize these signs can respond to peer pressure by saying, "I can't do that, my parents will know l did drugs."*

♦ *To help RECOGNIZE someone who has a substance abuse or medical problem. Studies report that children begin abusing substances two years before their parents ever know about the problem. The earlier a problem is recognized, the less damage will be done to the child and the family. Also, a child who is made aware of these signs can recognize others in their environment who may be impaired. This may be very important to a teen who is getting a ride from a party where alcohol or other drugs may have been shared illegally and wants to confirm the driver is safe.*

♦ *To help those who have a substance abuse problem to be RESPONSIBLE for remaining drug-free. The former user can request an eye check if they feel someone does not trust them. The concerned authority, family member, or friend can keep accountability high and help the former abuser by checking his/her eyes on a regular basis.*

Searching for Evidence needs to be a Parental Responsibility!
Do not overlook evidence that is abnormal.

If you have reasonable grounds to believe that your child is involved with alcohol or other drugs, you have the right and the responsibility to go through your child's belongings in search of hard evidence with which to confront them. However, you should show your children and teenagers the same respect as the law, in general, shows you. A police officer may not come into your home and go through your belongings without probable cause and a search warrant.   Similarly, you should not make a routine habit of searching your children's belongings.

One reason that searches are sometimes justified is that it's almost impossible to find out whether teenagers are involved in alcohol or other drugs by asking them. Often, when a child is confronted by a parent or authority figure and asked about his/her involvement with drug use, this only presents an opportunity for the child to lie. Lying is one of the most damaging aspects of the drug dependence process. Such behavior can cause an immediate loss of trust and, if not dealt with properly, begin a game of hide and seek which can destroy a family. While the truth may be difficult to deal with, it is always easier to handle than lies and distrust. Children will often lie if they feel that physical or emotional harm will be the result of their telling the truth. Our children should always know that we do not exist to hurt them, but to help them deal with the problems in life which they may encounter.

"I wish we had known all of these things when Tommy was around," Ann sighed then took a deep breath.

"Honestly, I never knew there was so much to this. We never had friends whose kids were on drugs. Or did we?" asked Bob. "Here comes the good part."

The moderator continued to deliver mounds of practical information that Bob and Ann were going to use in their ministry to other parents. Following is extremely pertinent information on what to do if drug use is suspected. How do you confronting a child or teenager about suspected drug abuse.

Parents frequently deny the evidence and postpone confronting their children. The earlier an alcohol or other drug problem is found and faced, the less difficult it is to overcome. If you suspect your child of using alcohol or other drugs, you must first deal with your anger, resentment, and sense of guilt. Do not take your child's alcohol or other drug use as a sign that you are a bad parent. Remember that parenting is not the only influence on a child's development.

In a two-adult household, it is essential that you present a unified front. Any disagreement between the two of you will be used by the child to deflect the issue away from their problem.

Do not try to confront your child while he/she is under the influence of a drug. Also, if your child is heavily intoxicated, do not make the mistake of allowing your child to "sleep it off." Take the youth to a detoxification center or a hospital emergency room immediately. Intoxication (alcohol or other drug poisoning) can have dangerous medical consequences. Therefore, it is of the utmost importance that your child be taken to a properly equipped medical facility, where he/she will be under the close supervision of qualified medical personnel. This action also sends the clear message that alcohol or other drug use is serious business and is not going to be taken lightly.

Another guideline to keep in mind during the confrontation is to act more and talk less. Parental lectures almost always fall on deaf ears when a child is already involved in alcohol or other drugs. The logical consequences that you devise and enforce will get your child's attention.

There are other Critical Guidelines for parental confrontation or intervention with you own children.

1. **Deal with your own emotions first**

Whether or not you can control your child, you can control your response to the situation and the child. Be careful not to react with rage or excessive anger. Although you may feel justified in becoming angry, a calm, firm response produces the best results. Trying to embarrass or humiliate your child will most likely be counterproductive. Bribery does not work. The child will accept the rewards, but continue to use alcohol or other drugs. Threats and unreasonable discipline tend to drive the child further into alcohol or other drug use.

2. ***Exit rather than explode***

   Sometimes you may be too upset with your child to deal rationally with the problem. By physically leaving the situation, you can keep from saying things you would later regret. Take a walk, yell and scream in a closed room, beat on a pillow, or call a friend to talk things out. Separating your emotion from the facts will help to increase the chances for success when you confront your child.

3. ***Listen without accepting excuses***

   There is a difference between listening to what children have to say and accepting their excuses. Rejecting their rationalizations and excuses enables both parent and child to deal with the real issue – the child's alcohol or other drug use. To accept those excuses (for your benefit or theirs) is to enable them.

4. ***Stand firm***

   It hurts to see your child hurt. But you must stand firm on your family's drug-free commitment. To allow your child's pain to compromise your views on the consequences of their behavior is to enable them.

5. ***Forgive***

   Parents and children alike need to know that there is hope – both for themselves and for their family unit. Once feelings have been appropriately expressed and consequences for the child's behavior have been applied, it is time for the relationship to be restored. Forgiveness is the first step in the healing process for both you and your child.

"Did we do anything right?" asked a bewildered Ann.

"Nothing I see here," Bob exhaled noisily.

"We did love Tommy, though. Even through all of the stuff he put us through, we always loved him," said Ann with a bit more confidence.

Later that afternoon, Bob was reading the paper and noticed an ad for a large house. "I'll be back in a minute," he told Ann and left. Bob and Ann had been married for over 40 years and had never made any significant or major decisions without talking about it. However, that day without asking anyone but the Lord, Bob bought the house on the spot. It would become well known as the Meadows House named after Ann's mom, Nellie Meadows.

Birth of Meadows House

Chapter Seven

"You did what?" exclaimed Ann.

"I bought a house," Bob said calmly. "In a little while we'll hop in the car and I'll show you."

"Wait a minute, Bob? A house? Why?" Ann was still stunned. For 41 years of marriage they had never made any major decisions without talking to one another.

"Ann, I just told the guy not to show it to anyone else because I wanted it," Bob was still trying to remain composed. "Its just too good of a deal for what I know the Lord wants us to do."

"But when you told him that, does that mean we're under some kind of an obligation to pay for it? Am I hearing this right? Have you actually decided that we are going to put in a residential treatment center," Ann asked. She was the type personality that did not move impulsively and needed all of the facts before she did. Bob's personality was almost the exact opposite. That's what had made the Wilson's such a good team.

"This is not a new idea, Ann. It's what we've been talking and praying about."

"Yes, I know. But, how are we going to pay for it," Ann continued to question.

"I have no clue," Bob replied almost under his breath. "If God wants it, it will happen."

Ann had never heard Bob make that kind of heart level statement, so she didn't say anything else.

Leading up to that unusual decision to purchase the house and, while Tom had been serving his six months Substance Abuse Felony Punishment program in the Texas Department of Criminal Justice, Bob and Ann had received their certification as Restorative Therapists™. They had both been doing hands on work with probationers and parolees in a counseling center, but were becoming somewhat frustrated by the lack of participation of those who had been mandated by Community Supervision to come to treatment and group and never showed up for their appointments. It was like pulling hound's teeth to get people to participate. After several meetings, Dr. Haynes and the Wilson's had come to the conclusion that the outpatient approach was not going to be as effective as they thought it would be with the addicted population they were trying to help.

"Listen guys," Michael said one day as a simple passing statement. "If God were truly in this effort, people would be coming to their sessions and groups. Actually, they would be coming out of the woodwork because of the program we are offering. They would be drawn to our ministry. Instead, we are having to chase them down most of the time. Something is wrong with this picture."

Of course, Bob and Ann were so new to substance abuse counseling that they thought what they had been experiencing was the norm. Nevertheless, they agreed in their spirits that he was right. Something was wrong.

"We are going to have to find a way to keep these people separated from their surroundings," he continued. "That probably means some type of residential treatment program."

With that statement and the coming together of several other circumstances, the seed was planted in Bob's mind and heart that a house where a few guys could live and be in a true faith based program away from their peers and enabling families was the way to go. He had casually mentioned it to Ann, but she didn't really let it fully sink in. Tom was serving his three-month stint after finishing his prison sentence in a half way house, which was a state run joke, as most of them are. He was working during the day at the out patient center and knew without doubt from an addicts point of view what had worked for him, and it wasn't the program they were trying to establish. Bob and his son had already had several discussions about finding something to rent or buy that would house a few men who were serious about their recovery, but all of this was only in the thinking and talking and looking around stages.

Then, one night at the half way house Tom heard a young man named Steve Neatherlin speak to their group. As Steve stepped to the platform in front of all of the other users and abusers, he opened with a simple introduction and then launched into his personal story.

"Why I am here in front of you is not about me," he said. "I know what I am about to say to begin my story is a little strange, but it is true! You see, I realize that my story is for His glory. I had nothing to offer Jesus when He called me. I was a junkie and a drunk. My life was driven by self and fulfilling the desires of my flesh! I started using drugs at nine years old. At the age of thirteen I actually started shooting up with a needle! My life got caught in a whirlwind of rebellion. My interest in school and future dreams dissolved, and I lived in an illusion daily.

Then, I began dealing drugs and that resulted with me using more and more. I quit school at the age of sixteen, and wound up married. I entered into the relationship with hurt, anger and with no trust. Needless to say, the marriage ended in divorce five years later. I spent most of my childhood life in an adult world without God! I have been arrested in this county alone seventeen times - all because my rebellious way of life.

I found myself feeling hopeless and had purposed to just end my life. Then, I began to drink and use drugs even more heavily thinking that would do the job and it would all be over. My pain would be gone. I was so bitter that I destroyed all of my relationships with fighting and finding fault. Then, one night, after shooting up some drugs, I was drawing and God's convicting power through the Holy Spirit moved upon my heart! My drawing transformed before my eyes and revealed to me that if I were to die at that moment, I would be on my way to Hell! Immediately, I went to the bathroom, fell on my knees and cried out to Jesus. I said, "Lord Jesus, forgive me and save me, because I don't want to die today and be in Hell!" That very moment I was radically changed! No church, no choir, just Jesus!! He came into my heart that very moment and I have never been the same.

Today, after some shaping and molding in my life, the Lord has me working with people who were just like me. I am now an ordained minister, a faith-based counselor and a loving father. What a difference Jesus can make! I've given my life to help others who have suffered and are suffering in the same manner as I did. My hope and desire is to extend God's Kingdom in a hurting world. I have totally surrendered to the call of God on my life, and in this, I have found meaning, purpose and peace. So, again, I came to realize

that there is more to life than what can be seen, that's why I know
today that it's not about Steve!"

In that short time, what Steve had to say deeply impressed
Tom. Some of the clients listened, some didn't. But that was
irrelevent. Tom listened and knew in his heart that what Steve had
said was right. They met afterward and found they had a great deal in
common. They had both been down so many of the same paths and
had made lots of the same stupid mistakes that abusers make. But the
most positive thing they had in common, which was different from
countless thousands of other people who were trapped in the drug
culture, was that they were serious about changing their lives and
becoming free from the bondage of dope.

The next day, Tom told Bob what Steve had to say and they
once again discussed some kind of a house or dorm or something
where they could take guys who were serious about changing their
ways and make a difference in their lives. All of these subliminal
incidents converged on the decision that Bob Wilson made that
afternoon when he saw the house. He knew in his heart that God was
leading his thinking, so he acted on pure faith like he had never done
before.

"Bob, we don't even have a program in place," Ann reminded
him.

"I know, but Michael said he would help us and there is this guy that spoke at Tommy's meeting the other night that he wants me to meet. We'll get it together."

Bob knew from his study of the DISC personality system that he needed to give Ann the support she needed because her strengths depended on having all of the facts prior to making decisions. Bob, on the other hand, usually just jumped out there and made things happen as he went. But this was different. This was God's business, and advancing His Kingdom was the real goal. So, he began to work on the details with her so that she could be kept informed.

Tom introduced Steve to his dad, and following an initial lunch meeting, Bob had his home director and the basis for the beginning of a program.

Steve Neatherlin and Bob Wilson at Meadows House

One evening after praying and discussing how they were going to start the facility, Ann said, "This is going to need more funding than we personally have."

"I know," Bob said. "Do you have a problem with us asking Nellie to help?"

Nellie Meadows, Ann's mom, had been blessed with provision from the Lord over the years and was exceptionally supportive of how her family was growing spiritually. She was also had a very special relationship with her Lord and was not the least bit hesitant when she knew that what she was giving to would help kids like her grandson, Tom. She only wished that the entire family would have seen and addressed Tommy's problem sooner. So, when she was asked for financial support to back the program, she stepped up to the plate and things were off and running.

Nellie Meadows at Counseling Center

After several meetings about programs, Bob, Ann, Steve, Tom and Dr. Haynes had the daily routine worked out and the house was named Meadows House after Nellie. She certainly wasn't looking for anything like that, but it was more than fitting. Plus, it was a great name for a treatment facility. Steve moved into the house as home director, the clients started coming and lives began to be changed.

Following and experiencing some start-up learning curves, word spread about the Meadows House and people even began to walk from other towns to be a part of the extraordinary things that was happening there. The team of highly gifted counselors and teachers fell into place and all had prayed that no one would be admitted to the program that God didn't send or want there. This stimulated a ground swell in the grass root grapevine that recovery could actually become discovery and that people could, in reality, overcome the deep-seated problems caused by addiction. Meadows House itself was surrounded by crack houses and indigent street people. It was like a beacon shining in the midst of an extremely darkened geographical setting. Several of the first clients that entered the program had to sleep on the floor with blankets. Then came the furniture and beds. Then came the food. God began to provide whatever was needed, whenever it was needed through the support of His people. Bob, Ann, and Nellie's church, Taylor's Valley Baptist Church, contributed in a myriad different ways. The guys began to do fund raisers at the local Sam's Club, Hollywood Video, and other stores, and with nothing but trust in God's grace, the Meadows House light began to shine even brighter.

Several newspapers wrote stories about how this semi-retired couple, Bob and Ann Wilson, came from knowing absolutely nothing about the world of drugs to a ministry of working closely with the dynamics of the chemically dependent.

One article was headlined, "Son's Experience Inspires Temple Retirees to Open Rehab Center." It went on to tell only the surface of the story, but Bob Wilson Ministries and Meadows House was on the map. Another feature article headline read, "Defeating the Scourge: Meadows House uses 12-Steps and the Bible to Stem Spiritual Wasteland of Addiction." It too touched only the superficial aspects of God's work, but served to spread the reputation successful recovery even further.

Bob formally yielded his life to the Gospel ministry and was licensed and ordained by his church. Tom, Tobby Zimmerman, Dr. Michael Haynes, Bob's pastor Jeff Loudin and several others taught and counseled on a weekly basis, and the six month curriculum was finally on track and on purpose.

One evening Ann asked Bob, "Do you think Michael would help us put together some sort of a newsletter? We need some way to thank the people who have supported us and to let more people know the program's needs. I know he's done that before."

"I'm sure he would. Just call and ask," he replied keeping his eye on the ballgame.

Ann and Michael began to work on the first Meadows House Newsletter called The Vision. This opened the door to let people know more about what God was doing through the agenda that He had obviously set into motion.

"We need to develop a statement of purpose, and put some of our treatment rules and goals in here somewhere," said Michael as they looked at the first draft. "Something like this."

Meadows House Purpose Statement

To provide people struggling with alcohol and drug problems the tools to regain control of their lives. To allow the individual to re-enter mainstream society through the use of these tools. To allow recovering people a treatment plan to recover their lives.

"The purpose statement needs to be simple. It will allow people to see in a thumbnail sketch what we are all about. Also, here are some things we might adopt as a motto. With a motto, we can start to build the image we want people to have of Meadows House,"

Michael continued. After some time of hammering out the words that best described what they thought God wanted to accomplish through the program, the house motto was placed in the front office for all incoming clients to see and read.

Meadows House Motto

We believe that there is nothing we have ever done or can ever do that God will not forgive.

We believe that no matter how far we might think we have strayed from the love of God, we can instantly make peace with Him.

We believe that God is much more interested in us living in our vision instead of living in our memory.

We believe that past mistakes cannot keep us from the unconditional love of God and our friendship with Him.

We believe that it is essential that we forgive ourselves for our faults in the same manner and to the same degree that God forgives us.

We believe that we are not perfect and are still a work in progress, so our desire is to make God our partner in our recovery and restoration.

We believe that there is nothing we cannot do for good and nothing is impossible if we put our total trust in God.

God was blessing what was happening at Meadows House. There really was no other explanation but God Himself. Now, Bob and Ann could not wait to get to the meetings and see the results of the spiritual labor that is flowing through them and all around them.

Ann remembered a statement Dr. Haynes made to her when Tom was sent to prison. "Out of the darkest night comes the brightest light." Once the Wilson's were aware that they were classic enablers and that enablers could kill addicts, this ministry has truly become their passion.

"Since we can't retire now," Bob said to Ann driving back home after a late night parent support group meeting, "I guess we'll just have to retread."

The Meadows House provides an atmosphere of home!

Tuesday Night Group with Jay   Thursday Night Group with Tom

The Case for Faith Based Counseling
Chapter Eight

In one particular FBCTI training course the Wilson's had attended, a professor from Houston named Baxter Castro Coffee presented his nationally acclaimed seminar, "I Can See Clearly Now." As Professor Coffee introduced his training, he made a strong case for the faith based counseling approach that was extremely inspiring to Bob and Ann. Baxter was a brilliant scholar, but he talked very softly and exceedingly fast. Consequently, the class had to listen especially carefully.

"History is on our side," Baxter said as he began to make his case for faith based counseling being a major player and having a rightful place in the treatment industry. "The historical evolution of the 'established treatment industry as we know it,' (ETI) is a dual testament of the progress in the fields of mental health and hygiene on the one hand; but on the other hand, serves as an indictment of its failure to significantly curb the epidemic of emotional and psychological discontent that permeates contemporary society.

If superstition and witchdoctors had been successful at treating mental illness, emotional disorders, addictions and behavioral problems, psychiatry would not have come into being. If psychiatry had provided all the answers, psychology wouldn't have come into being. If psychoanalysis, behaviorism, humanism, rational-emotive and cognitive therapy had all the answers, there would have been less need for transactional analysis, gestalt therapy, drug therapy, 12-step and group therapy programs. Had all, or any of the above established themselves as exceptionally capable of successfully addressing every issue, the multitude of holistic, nutritional, New Age, and self-help programs would not have evolved into the major industries they are today. In other words, the history of the **ETI** *indicates there is no single, all-inclusive discipline that can claim to successfully treat all the symptoms, of all the clients, all the time.*

In the absence of any such "all-inclusive discipline," **faith-based counseling (FBC)** *asserts its rightful place as a valid alternative to* **ETI***; and makes this claim on the strength and testimony of the millions of individuals who have benefited from the healing power of the eternal principles it teaches.*

Although the **ETI** *and* **FBC** *differ in their approach, the desired outcome is essentially the same. Both desire to assist the client in fulfilling their most essential needs while simultaneously coming to grips with reality. There has been much written about the differences between the* **ETI** *and* **FBC***, but in actuality there are some similarities. The recognition and acknowledgement of these similarities should encourage the* **ETI** *to be more accepting of* **FBC***, and* *empower faith-based counselors with the knowledge that **FBC** works; not just because it's done in the name of the Lord, but because the eternal principles that underlie all of the healing process are spiritual and intangible in nature. Medical doctors readily admit that medicine does nothing more than facilitate the body's healing of itself, a miracle by definition. And in the long run, psychologists merely guide the client back to all that is real and true; back to reality, back to themselves by giving up all that which is false and untrue – the same objective as **FBC**.*

*Contemporary members of the **ETI** believe that the root of all discontent is man's inability to meet his most essential needs. Many psychologists believe that at the top of this list is the need to love and be loved. The foundation of all **FBC** programs is the love of God, self and others; the essence of the "…two great commandments."*

*The **ETI** identifies the critical need for a client to feel worthwhile to themselves and to others. **FBC** has demonstrated that these needs can be significantly met when a client feels they have a greater sense of who they are, where they came from, why they're here and where they're going; coupled with the peace that comes from accepting responsibility for their thoughts and actions. They can confirm their sense of worth to others through   **FBC's** emphasis on serving God, family, country and the community. The **ETI** assists the client in understanding the perils and pitfalls of denying reality in their unsuccessful effort* to fulfill their needs but offer no real solutions. **FBC** offers the life changing solution by teaching that only the truth (that which is real, true and eternal) will "…set you free," Baxter continued. "I have heard Dr. Michael Haynes teach that FBC begins with the belief system and helps the client to discover and replace the lies they are believing with the following premise in mind. 'People do what they do because they believe the way they belief. FBC attempts to treat the roots, not the fruits'

The principle difference between the two disciplines is that the **ETI** focuses its efforts on the behavior of the client. **FBC** focuses its efforts on the heart and soul of the client with the belief that if these two are on track, the mind will become teachable, inappropriate behavior will become less desirable, and the client will begin to hunger and thirst for that which is real and true. In other words, the client will seek to live righteously.

Both the **ETI** and **FBC** guide the client through the therapeutic process. However, in the **ETI** it's the therapist that provides the guidance and direction, but with **FBC** the client is encouraged to seek guidance and direction from the Lord. The client seeks this guidance and direction in order to find **the way** to **the truth** in order to have **the life** we all deserve – a life that is meaningful and one filled with peace, love and joy. The "way" for one individual could be a major paradigm shift or instantaneous conversion filled with clarity and insight. For another it might come slowly, "…line upon line, precept upon *precept;" and for another the "way" might lead in the direction of more traditional forms of treatment, i.e. a substance abuse center, anger management classes, 12-step programs, group therapy, etc.* **FBC** *encourages the client to trust the "...still small voice" within them because that which is of God will never hurt them, or lead them astray.*

In one respect, **FBC** *has a decided edge over the* **ETI***, and this stems from the sheer magnitude of problems facing many of our souls-at-risk. One of the reasons that traditional forms of treatment have been less-than-successful in treating chronic substance abusers, the homeless, and former offenders isn't because most of their methods aren't valid, but because of the quantity of symptoms their clients display. Symptoms such as low self-esteem, self-destructive natures, explosive anger, paranoia, hostility, manipulative and controlling actions, etc. The scope of root causes behind these symptoms are seldom discovered and discussed by the* **ETI***. Maladies such a dysfunctional families, absentee parents, chemical imbalances, physical, emotional and/or sexual abuse, and many more root level life controlling issues and the behaviors they create such as substance abuse, sexual abuse, criminal activity, poor work habits, poor study habits, and more are many times left out of the treatment process. Much of the* **ETI** *only wants people physically sober. In essence, there are so many factors working against most clients who seek help that many would concur that it would take a "miracle" to salvage these populations. Please consider that* *miracles come from God, not men and programs. Whether the vehicle is medicine or prayer, the ultimate source is really the same.*

Since "miracles" fall into the realm of religion and not the sciences, **FBC** *becomes the more apparent choice when working with some populations of people who suffer from life controlling problems. Just because the miraculous must largely be accepted by faith, doesn't make it any less real than anything else that is abstract, unseen and not comprehensible to all, i.e. infinite galaxies, sub-atomic particles or quantum physics, or gravity.*

In closing, faith-based counseling represents itself as an alternative to, not a substitute for, the established treatment community's approach to wholeness. **FBC** *acknowledges that clients with serious substance abuse issues will still need the critical care of a detoxification facility, and clients who pose a threat to themselves or others may need their doctor, counselor, or pastor to refer them to a reputable mental health care provider. It is the position of* **FBC** *that its efforts are grounded in that which is real, true and eternal; and just because its approach may be less clinical, does not make it less probable. And just because unbelievers find it improbable, does not make it unworkable or impossible. The Lord said, "…With God all things are possible." Our mission isn't to try and explain how it works, but to demonstrate that in fact it does work.*

"I need to hear that again," whispered Ann to Bob when the class took a break. "I hope he has this written down somewhere."

"He's simply saying what Michael teaches in a little different way. He says that the faith based counseling approach deals with the three parts of man while the established treatment industry only deals with two and doesn't even believe in a third," said Bob. "This is what we learned in the first course. Man is three parts, body, soul and spirit. Not just two; body and soul."

"I remember," she relied with a slight smirk. "We must deal with the roots and not the fruits. We hear this all the time."

"He is also saying that faith based counseling concepts and principles have been around a lot longer than the established treatment industry," Bob continued. "Didn't in one of these classes that psychology, as we know it today, is only a product of World War II and Jesus was called mighty counselor over 700 years before he was born?"

"He did," Ann said as they began to move back to their seats.

At the end of that day, Dr. Haynes closed the class. "When a person with over 30 years experience in a supervisory capacity of a state agency that oversees thousands of convicted felons who have been released from prison through probation and are now residing in their respective communities stands before a group of ministers and says that The Department of Corrections and Community Supervision is a joke, it tends to get your attention," Michael said with such boldness that it startled the group. "This particular state level executive was actually asking a group of ministers and faith based counselors and organizations to help them try to deal with the tremendous numbers of substance abusers in the area. He frankly admitted that their established treatment programs were not working and were being shut down by the prison system due to budget shortfalls."

Michael went on, "When our now president, George W. Bush, was the governor of Texas, he put a task force of 14 church and government leaders in the field to find out why faith based counseling organizations and treatment centers were having three to five times the success rate than the state funded secular programs. Their report was titled **'Faith In Action…A New Vision for Church-State Cooperation in Texas.'** I have a copy of that report and I want to read one thing that this task force concluded," he said as he held the booklet up and allowed everyone to see the title.

" This is an opening quote. *'Government can hand out money, but it cannot put hope in our hearts or a sense of purpose in our lives. It cannot bring us peace of mind. It cannot fill the spiritual well from which we draw strength day to day. Only faith can do that. Signed Governor George W. Bush.'* End of quote," he alleged, as he looked everyone in the eye to make sure they got the point.

"Guys," he persisted, "this report was submitted to the Texas legislature in 1996, and as a result a law was passed to free faith based adult chemical dependency programs from the strict medical model of addiction and outrageous and unworkable rules of the Texas Commission on Alcohol and Drug Abuse. TACADA funded programs prohibited their counselors from even mentioning Jesus or God or faith or anything that had to do with spirituality. When House Bill 2481 was passed in 1997, things in the substance abuse treatment industry began to drastically change. Now, since George W. Bush has gone to Washington, Faith Based Community Initiatives have taken off all over the country. It is so sad that many state agencies don't even know about what the legislators did when they passed that law."

After the class was over, Bob stayed a little late to ask Michael if he would loan him the report so he could take it home and digest its obviously awesome significance. As he was looking through the recommendations, he was deeply moved by what the task force had suggested for the government to do. There were several sections, but the Wilson's were particularly interested what the recommendations said about substance abuse programs. Although the already knew, they wanted to make sure that Meadows House was on solid footing as far as the community and the law was concerned.

"Listen to this, Ann," Bob said as he read the title of section 4 on Combating Substance Abuse and Crime. "The state is trying to enlist the 'faith-factor' to promote a safer Texas. And this was released in 1996. Talk about just warming a pew, I'd never even heard of anything like this being done in our legislature. Furthermore, I'm quite sure that churches by and large don't know anything about it."

"I know," she responded with increasing interest.

He started reading some of the content, knowing she would read it all when he put it down, *"...The crisis of drug abuse is real, and we need to enlist the aid of effective live allies. Texas law, however, crowds out valuable faith-anchored programs by refusing to make room for their unique nature and philosophy."*

"Wow!" Bob exclaimed under his breath. *"Texas law embraces a strict 'medical model' of addiction. If you want to offer treatment in Texas, you must employ only professional licensed counselors with a certain academic pedigree and comply with numerous other strict requirements."*

"You know, Dr. Haynes has been saying this all along, but I never really gave it much thought as to how many holes addicts could fall into in this secular treatment process," Bob said.

"Michael has always referred to this system of counseling as a 'crocheted bathtub' that wouldn't and couldn't hold water. I never really knew what he meant, but it all seems to make sense now," Ann responded. "What we are doing in our program is actually changing lives and is not just a revolving door based on sheer economics. I'm more convinced than ever that this so called established treatment industry does not want people to be cured or healed. That would take away from their funding. Man!"

"Well, It humbles me to know we are truly a part of something this big," said Bob. "Just wish we'd started sooner. Nevertheless, now is better than never," he continued to read out loud.

"…By exhibiting a strong sense of credentialism and dismissing faith based efforts as 'amateurish', Texas law and regulations deprive many addicts a proven way to escape their destructive lifestyles"

Ann was glued. "I am not believing this! Before this bill was passed, the state was pouring millions of dollars down a black hole."

"What a hoax. A few people were getting filthy rich off of other people's pain," sighed Bob. "And we were right in the big middle of this scam with the life of our son in the balance. This makes me furious!"

"…But, results matter," the report said. *"And just as we respect results, we should respect the methods that achieve them. Texas should focus on programs that work in combating drug abuse. As our State focuses on outcomes, not process, we should celebrate good programs and dismantle the secular bias that crowds out their valuable work."*

As Bob and Ann lay in bed late that Saturday night before Easter Sunday Morning, Bob whispered, "I wish some of these legislators could be in church tomorrow morning so they could see the results of what a single faith based treatment program can do in the lives of people."

"Me too. But the really important thing is that God sees it," Ann whispered back.

"As usual, she's right," Bob thought but didn't say anything. He could not get over the fact that he was going to baptize six men whose lives were once shattered and scattered by their addictions and depraved choices. Now they had a chance for a new beginning. He was watching the change that was coming about in their lives on a daily basis from their involvement in the Meadows House program. Further he was astounded just to be a small part of the growth and development of each one of them. "Talk about results," he silently reflected.

Bob Wilson Baptizes a Meadows House convert

As Bob made his way into the baptistery on Easter Sunday morning, he looked out at the huge overflow crowd. This was the first Sunday in the new auditorium of Taylor's Valley Baptist Church.

"What a way to begin a service on resurrection day," he whispered not knowing if the microphone was on or not. This was the first time he had baptized anyone, but since he had been a part of leading these men to Christ during their recovery, the pastor asked him to perform the rite. He was experiencing apprehension and peace at the same time and was emotionally overwhelmed by the simple fact that he was even standing there. He kept repeating his lines, "I baptize you in the Name of the Father, Son, and Holy Spirit...I baptize you in..."

"What a privilege – an honor! " he thought. All sorts of things were swirling through his mind. Then it came time and the lights dimmed as the first of the six entered the water with him.

The first of eight to be baptized was Bob C. He was 40 years old and had been using drugs since he was 13. He spent several years in prison and had lost his family and had nothing but a small bag of clothes when he walked through the Meadows House doors.

"Bob, have your received Jesus Christ as your personal savior?" Bob Wilson asked. "I sure have," he beamed.

"Then I baptize you in the name of the Father, the Son, and the Holy Spirit."

As Bob began to lay him back, he took in some water and splashed a little bit over into the choir loft. But, everyone was so thrilled, a resounding AMEN echoed through the new auditorium.

They continued to come. There was Kevin who was 26 years old and had lost the chance to become a professional baseball player because of his addiction. Then there was Byron who had made a drastic change in the few months he had been in the Meadows house program. So drastic, that his parents could not believe what they witnessed as he went into the sacred waters. There was Tommy Lee, John, a former artist, and Dale who had been a raging crack addict until he was introduced to the Lord and began to work with his problem on a root level in his inner man.

Every one of these men and many more had been drawn to Meadows House in miraculous ways. There was even an 80-year-old alcoholic named Roy who had successfully gone through the program and was now on his own and happier than he had ever been in his entire life. Jay, a former hard-core biker and addict, had risen to a leadership role in the program and had surrendered his life to help others who were in the same bondage that he had trapped him. Jake, a preachers kid and Bible College student, who had gotten hooked on methamphetamine heard about the program from his dad who was a pastor in Ft. Worth and was miraculously drawn. There were so many others who had come through the Meadows House doors never to be the same. Some became casualties who were not really ready to own their stuff and take responsibility for their behavior left, but they were by no means the majority. The program was designed to be strict, but abounded with grace and not works. Therefore, there was always mercy at the house 'court of appeals,' but no one mistook that for weakness – just love for one another.

Sometimes it was 'tough love,' but always love and always personal. Meadows House clients were not numbers. They were real people and treated with true dignity and respect. Even the vast majority of hardened addicts were responding to that approach.

After the service had ended, Bob and Ann Wilson pulled up in front of Meadows House with some food for a couple of the guys who had been sick and not able to go to church.

Tears began to slowly swell in Bob's eyes as he looked at the sign in front. He was unashamed of their presence or if anyone even noticed **Meadows House: A Faith Based Drug And Alcohol Treatment Center: Bob Wilson Ministries, Inc.**

"Thank you God for not giving up on me over all of the years I ran from my call," he prayed as he and Ann got of the car. "How could we ever give up on any one?"

He echoed the prayer that he, Dr. Haynes, Steve, Tom, Angie, Nellie, Marj and Ann had prayed as they opened the program. Send us who You want us to help, we'll be here."

Meadows House Mania
Chapter Nine

Please understand that the personal testimonies of addicts are very similar. The devastation they leave in their wake of addiction is also extremely analogous or parallel. The burned bridges with the families and friends, the shame, the guilt, the unbelievable pain they shoulder in their daily lives, the evil and darkness they feel when they lay their heads on their pillows at night – is almost all comparable. There is a very intense resemblance to what addiction does to people's lives. However, the people themselves are as unique and different as the diversity of God. Their talents, backgrounds, appearances, families of origin are as different as night and day.

You see, dope knows no boundaries. Dope doesn't care where you live, how much money you have, what color your skin is, how much you weigh, whether you are pretty or ugly, or anything else about you. Dope is an equal opportunity tormenter.

Tom is doing great following his short stint in prison. Early during his incarceration he knew that he didn't want to use dope ever again. He never wanted to go back to that madhouse for the rest of his life. So, he learned all he could about the battlefield for the mind and how the dynamics of the renewing of the mind actually happened.   He is extremely serious about his recovery and is an associate director at Meadows House.   He works with people who have chemical dependency problems on a daily basis. Although he is has a new family, he is steadily making progress in repairing his relationship with his daughters Kayla and London.

Tom and his daughters London and Kayla

Tom and Angie Huggins were married shortly following his release from prison and they now have a new son named Brady.

Tom, London, Kayla, Angie, Brady

Tom has been given a brand new start in life and he is taking advantage of it. For the first time in years, he is a happy man who is giving back to his family and his community. God is in the process of restoring the years that the locusts ate during his drug use.

The Meadows House is gaining a reputation for being able to effectively help addicts change the direction of their lives. The program is so successful that the house now has a waiting list and people sleeping on the floor just to be involved what God is so obviously blessing. Just listen to some of the testimonies of the **Meadows House Family.**

My name is Mike M. Age 37 Background – Musician; Street Person; Prison
I have been a drug user for many years. I started using marijuana at age 8 and in only 5 short years I went from pot to meth to cocaine to heroin. By the time I was 16 years old I was a full-blown IV drug user. Finally, one year I was in a motel room on Christmas Eve. I had pretty much burned all of the bridges with my family and friends and had no one left. I found my self alone. I had been in Temple for a number of years and the streets where the Meadows House is now

located were the streets I used on. I had been in numerous programs that weren't faith-based programs. I knew Jesus, but I relapsed constantly because I wasn't letting it go and letting Him take over my life. I had been to churches, but a lot of churches don't know how to deal with addicts and they only tried to help my spirit and not my flesh. Then, they would send me out. God has me at Meadows House so that I can be treated in every area of my life. My body and my cravings, my soul and my spiritual life. If the Meadows House had not been right smack dab in the middle of the enemy's camp, I wouldn't have found it. I would have never listened to God's direction to come here. At first, I didn't understand how much my spirit needed to learn. Now, I see that it was an awesome thing for me to be able to see my three parts and the real roots of my addiction problems. Another thing about Meadows House is the counselors, both staff and volunteer. They are the best I have ever seen in dealing with the source of the chemical dependency problem. This gives us a wide of variety of people we can relate to. Also, the house is like a family. We all depend on each other.

Mike K. Age 32. Background - Good job; recreational user at first; good family

I have used drugs since I was in the 5th grade. I started with inhalants and then went to marijuana. I escalated to narcotics. I was a functional user. I had a good job and supported my own habits. Finally, a strong inner conviction came upon me that I was lost and headed to hell. Without turning my life over to God, I would be lost forever. I had to change. I went to a ministry here in Temple, but I knew right away it was not where I needed to be. I heard them talking about a man they referred to as Stevie Wonder. On a fundraiser one day, I walked by Meadows House and the man I was with said that was where Steve was. So, I left that facility and was drawn to Meadows House. I had left my job and sold my car. I wanted to meet Steve and that was all it took. Today is my 30th day in the program. When I first came into the house, I thought I might have made a mistake. But when I began to listen to the teachers, started working the program and met the guys, I realized that God had truly led me here so I settled down and began to learn. Now, I can say that the decision to stay and see this through was the best thing that I could have ever done with my life. I have learned so much about myself and why I did some of the stupid things I did. There is no doubt that I will remain here through the duration of the program. I want a changed life, and I believe I can get what I need at Meadows House. Thank God for this place.

Ben A.   Age   28.   Background - Good family; Musician; Anger problems

I started out early on with chemical abuse. I had a lot of hurts that I didn't know how to deal with as a young boy. I used almost as a child because I wanted to find love. I wanted attention and love. Then I became hooked and dependent on chemicals of all different kinds. I had given my life to the Lord when I was 5 years old at a conference. But that began a pattern of getting up and then falling down. No one taught me to stand up in victory, so my down times became longer than my victory. I spent my teens in sorrow and pain because I felt I could never make it. I became deeply ingrained in failure. I prayed and prayed and called out to the Lord to save me. I am a musician and songwriter and I can truly say that almost every single song I wrote something about, "Son of God, want You rescue me!" I can say today that God is faithful. When He makes a covenant He does not turn away. He went to everyplace I went and watched over me and continued to call me. I got married and have been married for 5 years to a Godly wife. She has seen me struggle with my addictions to drugs and I got to the point that I no longer feared death. I overdosed twice and that in my mind was a warm hand and a friendly thought because the devil had deceived me to that degree. Most of the pain was coming because I was estranged in my relationship with the Lord. I knew it, but I had bought into the lie that I was a failure and could not make it. Close to the end so many tragic things happened. Then I went to my mother and my step dad to get them to help me find some sort of treatment place because I knew I was about to die. I can remember sitting in my truck during the days wasted as I could be. I got wasted and listened to music. One day the Beatles came on with A Long and Winding Road and it broke my heart. I started crying and praying to God for this to be the last time for help. I told Him I could not go through this anymore. I literally begged God to get me somewhere to save my life. While I was sitting there, a card fell out of my wallet or seat, I don't know. But it said, "God is close to the broken hearted." I knew he was speaking to me and a little ray of hope began to grow again in me.

A couple of days later I prayed and asked God for a place to go to. I asked Him to lead me to which treatment center I could put my self into. I need help desperately. My step dad knew Dr. Haynes so he called him and he told him about the Meadows House and Bob Wilson. My step dad told me this was the place, but I didn't know yet. I called Mr. Wilson and after that conversation I was filled with such peace I was ready to go. When I entered the front door I can tell you that I knew immediately that Meadows House was and is filled with the spirit of God. Everything that has been set up here is filled with God's touch. Something extremely unusual hit me as I came in that door, and I knew I was in the right place for me to get the help I needed. I have been in the program for a month and I have learned more here and heard from God more in this place than ever before in my life. Sometimes through the day, I will be wrestling with something and then I will go to a class and 'boom' – there is the answer. I am totally blown away and excited about life and my music more so now than ever before. What a blessing. The strongholds that have kept me away from knowing God in a personal way are being pulled down daily. God is living through me now. I am not caught up in works and my own flesh anymore. Many may be skeptical and think it can't happen that fast. Oh yes – it can. I am living proof. Thank God I found this place. God bless Meadows House. Through this house, the guys and the program, God is breaking the lies that I was believing that had almost killed me. This is the place to be.

Kevin P. Age 26. Background – Semi professional baseball player with promising career.

I started drinking when I was 13. Every drug I have ever done I did because I was drunk. I had a promising baseball career going when I was 17 and then I started using cocaine. By the time I was 20 I was doing everything on the streets. Numerous drugs of all kinds consumed my entire being. Cocaine was my drug of choice until I was 24 and then came mushrooms. I found Heroine when I was 25 and stopped myself before I became physically addicted to it. I was drinking everyday and got drunk everyday. Then I began to literally eat tons of Zanax with beer. The first time I took Zanax I was gone for a week. I slept through Christmas and I had never missed a Christmas before.

I had been in a recovery facility before at another place that was supposed to be a faith-based, or Christian program, but found there were more drugs flowing there than even on the streets. My counselor told me about the Meadows House. I relapsed while in that program and was kicked out. I called Meadows House and wound up here as a last shot at getting clean. The difference in the Meadows House program and the others is that it gives me recovery and I still get to do life. I don't just sit in classes and then am not supposed to do anything else. At Meadows I can do my work, get my classes and learn how to do life normally. Just to be trusted has changed my life and given me hope. I know these people care about me and that too has given me back my hope for a future. Where the Meadows House is located, it would be real easy to just step out the front door and drink or use. It's all around us. But, I don't want to do that anymore. My want to got an overhaul at Meadows House. It's just different from other facilities. There is just so much God inside the walls of the home. It is very clear and present. It is a family atmosphere. People get involved with this program instead of just showing up to teach a class and getting their check. The people here have a genuine care about the clients and each other. Having someone show you that they really care about you is a life-changing thing for an addict.

Jake P. Age 25 Background – Preachers Kid; Called to Ministry at early age; Father was a Southern Baptist Pastor with The North American Mission Board in Alaska; Had Bible College Training.

I felt like I was called to the ministry at age 12 and began to take courses to prepare myself. I began to preach and teach youth Bible studies and do all the right things to learn about church work. I was a big advocate for the "True Love Waits" movement. From 1998 to 2000 I attended a Bible college in North Carolina and took graduate courses from several other seminaries. I moved to Ft. Worth in 2000 to be with my family. My father is a pastor. Shortly following that move I dated a young lady for 9 months and then married. My marriage only lasted for 5 months, which devastated me. When my marriage fell apart I resigned from the church but was at a loss as to why I couldn't hold my family together. Everything in my life prior to that time had gone very well and I could not understand what was happening. While I was going through this time some guys I hung with at my work introduced me to 'meth' and I started partying with them when my wife left. I had a son on the way and I just couldn't handle it. I withdrew from the church and thought my ministry was over and God had abandoned me. My mom and dad tried to be there for me but couldn't deal with me when I was high. The deeper I went into the drug world the less time I had with my family. We were once extremely close, but I was for all practical purposes just disappeared in the streets.

I was divorced at 21 and from 22 to 25 was nothing but heavy, heavy drug use. I started working in bars as a bouncer and virtually lost my past identity. I had no way to make money so I started manufacturing and distributing 'meth.' My whole life had been taken over by darkness it seemed like. At the beginning of 2005 I knew I couldn't live this way anymore, but I felt trapped. I thought I had buried my family or myself so deep I couldn't get back to God. I tried to commit suicide but failed. I deliberately put myself in situations where I should have died. I have been shot and stabbed.

Then, last Thanksgiving one of my dad's church members told him about Meadows House. She talked to me about Meadows House for about a half hour. She knew I needed help and I was admitting to myself that I did. After that, anytime I would even attempt to pray, the Meadows House popped into my mind. I felt like I had burned all of my bridges and I knew I needed to began to pull away from the users I hung out with. I literally became homeless. I couldn't live on the streets and I couldn't live at home. I had never even heard of Temple and I felt like this was to big a leap and a truly impossible thing. One night I was at the end of my rope and went to my dad and asked him to call the church member who had told us about Meadows House. We called on a Thursday night and Steve was teaching. They told my mom that they would return the call in the morning. I spent a little time with my family and was on my way back out. I felt like I had given the Lord a try and it didn't work. I knew I could go back to the dope house because I would immediately have money, so I resigned myself to the fact that I had blown it so bad that dope would be my calling in life. It went against every moral thing that had been instilled in me and I knew it was totally wrong, but I had run out of options.

However, on my way back out Steve called and said he felt like the Lord was telling him to get in touch with me. My mom literally caught me by my backpack and pulled me back into the house. She talked to Steve for about 15 minutes then I talked to him. I cried, broke down and told him everything. He identified. He said he just wanted to find out if I really wanted to do the deal and get clean. The next morning, I was on a bus to Temple. I have been at Meadows House for three months and the Lord has literally turned my life around. My dreams are back. My hope has returned. I can see opportunities for ministry and am actually doing ministry while in the program. It is an awesome thing and a truly awesome place. I feel I have been given my life back.

In July of 2003, Bob and Ann Wilson went through The Faith Based Counselor Training Institute courses and became certified as Chemical Dependency Counselors and Restorative Therapists. They also became certified Personality Profile Consultants. Following that, they began their ministry to the addicted. It was during that time that their son was in prison. But they wanted him to join them when he finished his sentence. He did! Tom went through the FBCTI training and became certified immediately upon his release. Ann was interested in groups and started with 3. Meadows House opened its doors in August of 2004 and the support groups have grown to over 50 people 3 times per week.

Local churches have come to the aid of Meadows House by supporting the program with furniture, clothing, funding and food. There were 2 people in residence at the start of the program. There are now 18 men in this unique recovery program and a large waiting list to get in. the guys in the house have started a lawn service and do fundraisers at businesses such as Sam's, Academy Sports, Hollywood Videos, Summer Fun, Wal Mart, and others. The musicians have started a band that has performed in several churches, conferences and even on parking lots. The Meadows House tee shirts have "Addicted to Jesus" on their backs.

There have been clients from 18 to 80 enter the program. All in all, people are beginning to call this incredibly successful residential faith based drug and alcohol treatment facility Meadows House Mania!

Meadows House Reference Guide For Parents

Chapter Ten

Appendix Information for Parents Who Are Experiencing Or Suspect Substance Abuse Problems With Their Children And Need Prevention Skills To Help Them To Walk Through a Drug Filled World Safely.

<u>Meadows House Reference Guide For Parents</u>
<u>Chapter Ten</u>

There may be people in our immediate family or people you know who have some sort of chemical dependency problem. The following pages contain information that Bob and Ann Wilson discovered on their journey from sitting in church behind stained glass windows Sunday after Sunday not knowing the ministry outside in the desperate and hurting world of drug abuse.

We hope this reference material may prove to be a valuable tool for teaching prevention to your children before you have the total family problem that substance abuse can cause.

Bob and Ann Wilson
Dr. Michael K. Haynes

RESPONSIBILITY

This section is designed to provide an overview of the basic responsibilities parents should assume to assure their child the opportunity to grow up drug-free. Areas discussed include:
- Understanding the Drug Problem
- Understanding the Adolescent
- Building Protective Factors (Resiliency)
- Recognizing Parental Roles
- The Power of Modeling
- Values and Spirituality
- Applying the Principles to Gateway Drug Prevention
  Parents and Prevention

The use of alcohol or other drugs among our youth continues to command center stage as the foremost problem affecting young people and their families. **Numerous studies indicate that**

parental attitudes and practices related to alcohol are the strongest social influence on children's use of alcohol or other drugs. Moreover, the nature of the interaction between parent and child has been found to be a key factor in predicting adolescent initiation into alcohol, tobacco, and other drug use. But parents need help. The widespread availability to both children and youth of alcohol, tobacco, and other drugs is a relatively new phenomenon, posing challenges that are in some ways unique to this generation of parents, many of whom are not yet aware of the significant role they can play in preventing alcohol, tobacco, and other drug use by their children.

It is important to recognize that parents in the general population:

- Believe that alcohol or other drugs are a national problem but may be unaware that their own children are at risk.
- May be unaware that their own children are exposed to alcohol or other drugs at an early age.
- May have little information about specific drugs and their effects.
- May find it difficult to talk to their children about drugs, sex and other dangerous issues.
- May accept limited drug use among adults.
- Usually abstain from drug use or excessive alcohol use.
- Believe parents should take the lead in preventing drug use by their own children.

Family - Then & Now

According to J. Howard Johnston, in his monograph "The New American Family and the School" (National Middle School Association, Columbus, Ohio 1990),
"Through the 1930's, 1940's and 1950's the average United States household contained approximately four people. It was the "typical family" of a working parent, a homemaker parent, and one or more dependent children. Indeed, even in 1960, sixty percent of all United States households were constituted that way. By 1980, however, only eleven percent of American households looked like that of 1960; by 1983 the proportion had shrunken to seven percent, and by 1988 estimated to be less than four percent. Now, the average size of a United States household is just over two residents. This means that many families are having to cope with a smaller "human resource" in managing necessary affairs such as generating income, providing child care, or caring for an aging parent."

Johnston goes on to report,
"At present, nearly fifteen percent of children are born out of wedlock, fifty percent of those to teenage mothers. And while the economic problems associated with teenage pregnancy and childbearing have not changed much in the past decade or two, the acceptance of this unwed mother phenomenon is growing, giving America the highest teenage pregnancy rate of any industrial Nation on earth. In fact, every day in the United States, forty teenage girls - a school bus full - give birth to their third child! By some estimates, as many as ninety percent of unwed mothers keep their babies, raising them themselves or with the help of extended families, such as parents, siblings, or close friends."

"But our family is different than the traditional."

There is no reason to believe that a non-traditional family, a single-parent family, or a reconstituted family is not perfectly capable of raising and nurturing healthy, happy and successful children. The problem seems to develop when families of any size, racial makeup or economic strata leave the addressing of these critical areas of concern to government, school or other social service and media institutions.

Understanding The Adolescent

Adolescence is a time of radical change. Change in the youth is understandable with powerful hormones being introduced to the body from evolving glands creating tremendous physical, emotional and mental pressures. Changes for the adult(s) during this period are less recognizable and yet very present. Accommodating the parental relationship to meet the changes in a youth is a difficult task. Also, the parents are continuing to grow and change as well. What seems to be a natural process is far from such. There is now no such thing as "normal" for this family.

It is important to note that children and adolescents have the same basic needs of all individuals. The need for survival, security, relationships, significance and love are very strong. The meeting of these needs in a manner that is socially acceptable and personally fulfilling is the task of parents. These needs actually become drives and will be acknowledged and fulfilled in some way! Properly meeting these needs and directing these drives can lead to a natural fulfillment. Out of control, however, these drives begin to take control of their host and others around them. Drug use, sexual activity, inappropriate aggression or other actions may result from improper meeting of these basic needs.

Parents and other caregivers have a significant task in monitoring these critical areas. While meeting these needs for the child, it is imperative that they also provide training for the child in their charge on how to best meet these needs on their own without turning to the use of chemicals or other negative consequence behaviors (drugs, gangs, sex, or violence.)

What Keeps a Child From Using Drugs?

Despite all the negatives associated with risk factors which contribute to the likelihood that young people will become involved in tobacco, alcohol and drug use, there is hope! Research in different countries has shown that a variety of factors help protect against negative risk factors. And the more of these factors that are present, the more likely the child will develop resiliency.

RESILIENCY is defined as *the ability to recover from or adjust to misfortune or change.*

Resiliency is what enables some children, not only to survive in the midst of adversity, but also do well in life. Resiliency encompasses factors and individual characteristics that make some children less vulnerable than others though they grow up in the midst of family problems, poverty, violence and stressful situations.

Protective Traits in a Resilient Child

Social competence includes qualities such as responsiveness, especially the ability to get positive responses from others; flexibility, including the ability to move between different cultures; empathy; communication skills; and a sense of humor.

Problem-solving skills encompass the ability to plan; to be resourceful in seeking help from others; and to think critically, creatively, and reflectively.

Autonomy is having a sense of one's own identity and an ability to act independently and to exert some control over one's environment, including the ability to complete a task and feel in charge. The development of resistance (refusing to accept negative messages about oneself) and of detachment (distancing oneself from dysfunction) serves as a powerful protector of autonomy.

Lastly, resilience is seen in having a Sense of Purpose and a belief in a bright future, including goals, direction, educational aspirations, achievement, motivation, persistence, hopefulness, optimism, and spiritual connectedness.

<u>What Can You Do As A Parent to Foster Resiliency in Your Child?</u>

- Establish close bonds in infancy
- Practice a high warmth, low criticism style of parenting
- Foster a sense of basic trust
- Be supportive and affectionate in your relationship with your child
- Expect success
- Provide structure, discipline, and clear rules
- Consider the role of a belief system in providing stability and meaning

Parents should provide opportunities for children to participate and contribute to the family in meaningful ways such as giving children appropriate responsibilities, providing recognition and rewards for newly learned skills, and teaching the skills necessary for healthy relationships.

ALCOHOL OR OTHER DRUG PREVENTION ROLES FOR PARENTS

In addition to serving their basic and more general roles as family leaders and nurturers of their children's development, parents can play a variety of specialty roles in helping their children lead drug free lives. These additional roles require that parents look closely at their own alcohol or other drug use, that they become knowledgeable about an array of alcohol or other drug use issues, and, most important, that they make a drug free lifestyle a major child-rearing goal. The intended result – drug free, healthy youth – is a blessing to the parents, their immediate and extended families, and the nation.

Concerned Parents Must Be:

Responsible Role Models

Parents are role models regarding the use of legal substances such as tobacco, caffeine, and alcohol and illegal substances such as marijuana, stimulants, sedatives, cocaine, and heroin. Parents model through their own alcohol or other drug use behavior and whether and how they involve their children in this behavior.

Educators

Parents must assume the primary responsibility of the education of their families about legal and illegal substances and their likely health and social consequences. Family health histories regarding alcohol or other drug use are extremely important to our children. Also, the pro-use messages that emanate from the alcohol or other drug industries, the media, and poorly informed health practitioners must be addressed. This educational role requires that parents become very knowledgeable and a share their clear no-use and no-sale family policies or rules with clear and enforceable consequences for violators.

Providers of Structure & Discipline

Parents are family rule setters for their children regarding the use and sale of alcohol or other drugs. The focus is on arriving at clear no-use and no-sale family rules with clear and enforceable consequences for violators.

Parents can also plan enjoyable family activities that provide alternatives to boredom, or social events involving alcohol or other drugs. The focus is on helping children engage in healthy activities, including alcohol- and drug-free parties.

Interveners

Knowing the signs of alcohol or other drug use and how to confront a child about the use of alcohol or other drugs is a significant responsibility. The focus is on how to handle children or youth who are dependent on alcohol or other drugs and where to refer them for treatment. This also involves parents being managers of their own feelings about their children's alcohol or other drug use. Parents must work through these feelings so that they can take productive remedial action.

<u>MODELING</u>

How do you handle anger, depression, rejection, weariness, frustration, failure, financial setbacks, death, job loss or other life issues? These life realities are the times when we provide some of the most important life lessons our children will ever learn. If these life crisis points cause us to blame, become physically or verbally violent, insulting, or turn to chemicals for relief, it may not be too surprising to see the same behaviors in our children. Children are receptors and reflectors. Recognizing that, every parent becomes painfully aware that some of the very attitudes and actions we don't like in our children are the same that we don't like in ourselves.

Athletic stars are condemned when they fail to be proper "role models" for children today. The truth is, they are really not the important role models that teach children how to handle life and its success or setbacks. They are heroes. Parents, teachers, neighbors, uncles and aunts, grandparents, coaches and others who spend time with them daily are the real "role models" for living. These teach them how to handle life by example.

Watch a child's eyes when a parent is confronted with a crisis point in life and the lesson is quickly driven home. They watch their parent – intently observing their every action and emotion. This is a "teachable moment" for certain.

The powerful lesson for parents in regard to the issue of modeling is simple. **Live what you want them to learn.** Parents often wonder why children pick up negative traits such as a "bad temper." They often do not realize that children indiscriminately imitate what they see. Parents may know that they model responsibility and other positive behaviors but are unaware that they model some negative traits as well. There is one person in the equation of parenting that you do have power over and that is yourself. If you do not desire for your child to be rude when angry, hold your tongue. If you want your child to set goals, share yours. If you don't want your child using chemicals to change their moods, bolster their courage, or kill their pain, then don't behave in that way. Children learn what we live.

MODELING ALCOHOL OR OTHER DRUG USE

The best defense parents and leaders of young people can provide is found in the way life is lived everyday. Drug prevention requires a close look at the attitude toward drug and alcohol use demonstrated in the home. Every child knows what will not be tolerated in the home and society. When young people see their parents and other adults using alcohol or other drugs heavily, they say, "Why can't I use?" As long as the statement of prevention is that "_some people_ can't handle this," the youth will test to see if he is one of those who can. Only a no-use message can protect children today.

Parents who drink alcoholic beverages, smoke, or drink a lot of caffeinated coffee may not think of these as drugs, nor do they always realize the influence these practices can have on their children. They may offer a child a sip of beer or wine at family parties and think there is no problem with drinking ☐ especially if they abuse alcohol. You can...

- Monitor your own use of drugs such as alcohol and prescription and over-the-counter medicines.
- Promote health by appropriate eating and exercise habits.
- Be consistent in your attitudes about drug-influenced behavior. (Many parents become incensed about alcohol-impaired driving but laugh at drunken behavior in a television comedy skit.)

- Explain when over-the-counter or prescription drug use is appropriate and inappropriate. When a child has a headache, for example, could a warm washcloth or heating pad relieve the pain? Many headaches are tension and stress related. You might ask the child about his/her day to see if something upsetting happened?
- Discuss television commercials that advocate the use of over-the-counter drugs. Find out what your child thinks the commercial is trying to say and solicit their ideas about the appropriate use of medicine and the other options available for common problems such as headaches, stomachaches, and insomnia.

MODELING THE EXPRESSION OF FEELINGS

A primary purpose of alcohol or other drug use is to alter emotions. Children need to learn not to be afraid of emotions and to express them in appropriate ways. An effective way to model the expression of feelings is to use an "I message."

An" I message" is a statement about the effects on the speaker of another person's behavior. A parent might say, "When I find mud on the rug that I have just cleaned, I feel discouraged because now it has to be cleaned again." The parent has not blamed the child but simply communicated his or her feelings about the consequences of the child's behavior. "I messages," coupled with reflective listening, help children learn to express their own feelings.

In reflective listening, the parent demonstrates an understanding of the child's feelings and the circumstances that cause them. The parent communicates this understanding in words such as these: "You feel sad because your friend is moving"; "Sounds like you're angry because I won't let you do that." Simple ways of communicating understanding are "you feel • because •, " "sounds like you're •," and "looks like you feel"

MODELING DECISION-MAKING

Using or not using alcohol or other drugs is a decision. Parents should teach decision-making as early as possible by allowing children to make choices consistent with their age and level of maturity. Decision-making begins with low-risk choices such as whether to have an egg or cereal for breakfast. Once the choice is made, the child is expected to accept the positive or negative consequences of the decision. With practice, the child learns to predict the negative consequences of decisions. This ability is especially important when deciding whether to engage in behaviors such as using alcohol or other drugs.

Parents can also teach decision-making by involving the child in decision-making processes. Exploring alternatives is a useful model for making decisions. You can model the process by using the following steps to help the child solve a problem:

- Use reflective listening to understand and clarify your child's feelings. Problems often remain unsolved if feelings are not expressed.
- Explore alternatives through brainstorming. Encourage creative thinking. Solicit the child's ideas without evaluating them.
- Help the child to choose a solution. Ask your child to evaluate each alternative listed in the brainstorming process.
- Discuss the probable results of their decision. Help your child examine the likely consequences of each decision. This is especially important when a potentially harmful behavior is being considered.
- Obtain a commitment from your child to follow through with the chosen solution.

189

- Plan a time for evaluation. The solution is tested for a specific period of time – a week, for example – and then discussed ("Shall we talk about how it's going next Tuesday?").

Parents are the primary role models of alcohol or other drug use, the expression and acceptance of feelings, and decision-making. These are areas, which have been found to be influential in a child's decision to use or abstain from using alcohol or other drugs. Parents must begin to exert their positive influence before the onset of peer pressure.

TEN POWERFUL PARENTING EXAMPLES

You can provide good models for your children by what you do and by what you avoid doing.

1. Show that you value your freedom to think and act independently – that you don't have to do something because "everyone is doing it." This helps your children see that unwanted peer pressure could be rejected.
2. Be consistent in your words and actions. For example: a phone call interrupts your dinner and you say, "Tell them I'm not home yet." The message your children hear is that it's OK to be dishonest for your own convenience.
3. Demonstrate your own sense of self-respect and self-esteem. For example, taking care of your health through exercise and diet offers a strong model for your children. Be creative and constructive in your use of free time, showing that there are alternatives to being a "couch potato" or "hanging out."
4. Show respect for your children's lives and concerns by being a good listener. Be sincere, ask questions and use a touch or a look for encouragement.

5. Be cautious in using prescription or over-the-counter medicines as a quick fix for pain or stress. Your example can help counter the media messages that discomfort can be cured by chemicals.

6. Be aware of how your own use of alcohol or other drugs can influence your children. Avoid using excuses for drinking or drug use, like having a rough day. Your drinking and drug use behavior tends to be the same behavior your children will have when they grow up.

7. Talk honestly about stress or conflict in your own life. Children need to know that such struggles are a natural and normal part of life. They have a good model when they see that you are coping with problems without relying on alcohol or other drugs.

8. If you are trying to change something in your behavior – such as quitting smoking or losing weight – be willing to talk about what works and what doesn't.

9. Demonstrate that spending time with your children is something you value and look forward to. If you are often too tired or too busy, they are likely to imitate your behavior.

10. Be open in showing that you love and value all members of the family.

CHILDHOOD ROLE MODELS
A Self-Evaluation For Parents

Role models are especially important to children between the ages of eight and twelve. Think about your own role models at those ages and write your answers to each question in the space provided. If you need more space, use a separate sheet of paper.

When you were your child's age, who were your role models? Make a list; then choose one to focus on. What was there about that person that you admired? As a child, what did you most admire about the way your parents – or one parent in particular – made decisions or handled a crisis?

Can you think of ways that you imitated the actions or habits of one of your parents? What special thing about yourself would you most like your children to imitate?

Values & Spirituality

Every family has expectations of behavior that are determined by principles and standards and their religious convictions. These add up to "values." Children who decide not to use alcohol or other drugs often make this decision because they have strong convictions against the use of these substances – convictions that are based on a value system. Social, family, and religious values give young people reasons to say no and help them stick to their decisions.

VALUES
Here are some ways to help make your family's values clear:

- **Communicate values openly**. Talk about why values such as honesty, self-reliance, and responsibility are important, and how values can help your child make good decisions. Teach your child how each decision builds on previous decisions as one's character is formed, and how a good decision makes the next decision easier.
- **Recognize how your actions affect the development of your child's values**. Simply stated, children copy their parent's behavior. Consider how your attitudes and actions may be shaping your child's choice about whether or not to use alcohol or other drugs.
- **Look for conflicts between your words and your actions**. Remember that children are quick to sense when parents

send signals by their actions that it's all right to avoid
unpleasant duties or to be dishonest.

- **Make sure that your child understands your family
values**. Parents assume, sometimes mistakenly, that children
have "absorbed" values even though they may be rarely or
never discussed. Discuss clearly why these are important to
you and why you choose to live by their direction.

SPIRITUALITY

*It is a proven fact that children who are actively involved in a
structured religious group have less incidence of negative
consequence behavior than those who are not. It is also worth
recognizing that the initial steps of most recovery programs
(12 Step Programs, etc.) guide the individual toward the
development of a spiritual life and recognize these steps as
critical to effective recovery. What is required for recovery is
certainly important in prevention.*

Families actively involved in religious groups find a foundation
for their beliefs and values that is supported and encouraged by
others. The strength they find in their faith and the fellowship of
support become vitally important factors in times of stress and
instability. The very realization that others are depending on them
cause young people to think twice about their behavior. The need to
belong and be accepted is often met by their religious group
involvement as well.

The parent of today who has a desire for their child to
discover the same support and comfort that they have known from
their God must not assume that the child will discover that source
without guidance. The assortment of religions and cults that confront
our children today can become more a source of confusion than
support without the help of their parents. When religion and

spirituality is not discussed, children will seldom introduce the subject to the parent. Sadly, even less than parents talk to their children about sex, gangs or even drugs do they discuss their spiritual lives with their children?

The facts are clear. Children with an internalized standard of right and wrong, a sense of a responsibility to God and others for their behavior, and a supportive fellowship with which to interact are far less likely to become a victim of alcohol or other drug abuse.

STEPS TO FUNCTIONAL PARENTING

Much has been written about the "Dysfunctional Family." While all families at some point become a bit "dysfunctional," it is helpful to look at how you can create a family that works. Here are a few ideas for you to get started in building a functional family. The earlier you begin, the more effective you are.

- Be objective & honest in evaluating your child. Do not cover weaknesses or wrongs.

- Don't allow your child to have privileges beyond his/her level of responsibility.

- Maintain a standard of personal responsibility for all their actions.

- Don't make rules that are not meant to be kept and don't back down when discipline may inconvenience you. FOLLOW THROUGH!

- Don't remove punishment for wrong actions without full application of consequence.

- Talk! Communicate! Find common interests or events to discuss. Let words flow between you. Acknowledge that they are important enough to listen to. Share your own ideas and dreams.

- EXPRESS FEELINGS – positive or negative – in acceptable ways. Share feelings of anger, doubt and fear to let your children see how you handle them. You are their primary example for future expression. Remember, **what we don't talk out we act out.**

- Let them know when you are extending the boundaries of your trust for them.

- Maintain a clear standard that showing responsibility will gain them more freedom and that displaying less responsibility will diminish privileges.

- Connect "yes" and "no" to "why." Logic for decisions does not always need to be defended but should always be expressed.

- Tell them the positives of what they can be and "are" every time you tell them what they did wrong or what they "aren't."

PREVENTION ASSOCIATED WITH SPECIFIC GATEWAY DRUGS

This section has provided you with elements that are essential to taking action and being a responsible parent and nurturer of a healthy family. The following section contains information to help you understand and relate your effective parenting skills to the prevention of gateway drug use by your child.

WHAT CAN A PARENT DO TO PREVENT ALCOHOL ABUSE?

Examine your own attitudes toward drinking and set a good example of no-use of any substance for mood alteration.

- Be consistent in teaching and personal practice.
- Communicate with your family about alcohol and the dangers involved in abuse using factual information. Education should begin early and continue through adolescence.
- Provide a means of handling peer pressure situations. Let them know that they need not apologize for not using and that it is not abnormal.
- Teach them ways to say "no" firmly and without explanation. Role-play situations with them to test their skills.
- State rules, expectations and consequences for the use of alcohol and follow through with promised discipline if they are violated.
- Explain the fallacy of the philosophy that "everybody does it" and "you have to drink to have fun."
- Refuse to be misled by "cover-up" and condoning statements such as: "It's not mine"; "It's only a little beer. It could be worse", and "I've only tried it once."
- Create a plan to provide transportation home in the event alcohol problems develop when the child is out with friends.
- Search out and participate in parent groups dedicated to abstinence for youth.

A CLOSER LOOK AT MARIJUANA PREVENTION

Marijuana use is not a victimless crime. Especially not when you consider the costs of health care and lost productivity resulting from it, or the suffering the typical user causes their family. These costs are usually borne by society as a whole and do not include the cost associated with impaired driving performance or of marijuana-related accidents on the job. In a society as interdependent as ours, self-destructive behavior is never victimless.

- Clearly state your family's rules against the use of any illegal drug and the consequences for violation. Repeat the message as the child grows older and enters new social systems.
- Recognize that a teen's use of marijuana is often their method of coping with pain, boredom and hopelessness in life. These problems often outweigh the known negative consequences of marijuana use. Look for signs of low self-esteem and boredom.
- If the home life of a teen is critical, negative, and boring, there will be an effort on their part to reach outside the home for excitement and acceptance.
- Teaching youth to avoid chemically induced highs in favor of natural highs that come from happy, fulfilling relationships and the attainment of realistic and inspiring, personal and family goals is a major drug deterrent. We do well to remember that children and teens have little concept of the future and are focused primarily on the "now". Parents must relate the present to future desires, goals and happiness.
- Learn about the drug and how it operates. Clearly explain the dangers of marijuana use. Emphasize the long-term effects and dangers. Youth find it hard to accept the dangers because they have so many friends who are seemingly unaffected by use.

Fight back against media and social messages that attempt to glamorize and socialize the use of marijuana.

INHALANT PREVENTION ACTION

- Read the labels of household products. Many household cleaners, paints, food dispensers, and other chemicals contain some form of a psychoactive drug. Check the content labels on available products, especially those used by youths. Ask your pharmacist for assistance.
- Be aware if you see a lot of empty containers of products in which you may question use by your child. For instance, fifth graders who have multiple empty bottles of "octane booster" (a car gasoline treatment product which is often used as an inhalant.)
- Be aware of missing regular household or office products that could be potentially abused by children. (Example: correction fluid, markers).
- Lock up and monitor all dangerous chemicals. There is no sense taking chances. Paints, cleaners, solvents and other chemicals should be put off limits without supervision. When using these chemicals, take the opportunity to instruct as to personal precautions and danger. The inconvenience is slight compared to the peace of mind.
- Maintain close supervision of children. A major similarity of abusers of inhalants is the lack of supervision. The interest shown by the concerned parent is valuable to the esteem of the child as well. Remember your own youth and how quickly temptation could turn to wrongdoing. Keep in touch throughout the day. Discuss daily activities at dinner. Not only do you have the right to know, you are responsible. Also, it lets the child know you are concerned about his life.
- Schedule the child's day. An old proverb says, "An idle mind is the devil's workshop." A child with something constructive to do finds boredom an infrequent problem. Learning to plan for the next day teaches a good habit for life. The child is not as

susceptible to peer pressure and has a reason to say "no" to those heading toward trouble when he has already made plans. The performance of daily plans also provides a sense of accomplishment. Get them a calendar.

• Watch for signs of use. Unfortunately, there is still the chance that experimentation might occur and lead to regular use. If so, quick response is imperative before major dependency occurs.

STEROID ABUSE PREVENTION

Note: Steroids are included in this section because of the potential for abuse by young people due to the emphasis on body form in our society. In some cases, steroids may be used by young people who would normally avoid the more common drugs such as tobacco, alcohol or marijuana.

• Educate all young people concerning the long-term dangers of steroid abuse. Use factual and explicit materials to communicate the dangers. Let youth know that you are aware of the signs of abuse.

• Emphasize the uniqueness and talents of every individual. Offset media emphases on physical perfection and strength as the main criteria for acceptance or success with high praise for non-physical achievements.

• Inform athletes of school and civil penalties for steroid use or sale and the effectiveness of drug testing procedures in detection.

• Establish parent information groups to share information with parents of athletes. Commend the efforts of any coach to refuse involvement with hormonal drug manipulation.

• Provide alternative methods of strengthening the body and mind for competition. Consider the nutritional,

psychological and mechanical areas of training along with the physical.
- Watch for signs of obsession with strength or a feeling of inadequacy due to physical weakness in children and teens.
- Consider medical attention for late-maturing males to avoid self-treatment by steroids.
- Encourage the de-emphasis of a "winning at all costs" attitude in all little league sports and a renewed emphasis on the joy of play and the pleasure of healthy competition.

PLACE YOUR PRAISE CAREFULLY

No arena in our society receives the level of praise and acclaim that sports figures experience. From the grade school to the professional levels the adoration bestowed upon successful athletes is unrivaled. Our society must give attention to the impact of such selective praise. Concerned educators and parents must actively pursue equal praise and acknowledgment of youth for mental as well as physical accomplishments. Steroid abuse begins with a distorted concept of acceptance that can be controlled by parents and leaders of youth.

CONCLUSION

Prevention is a lifestyle. The role of the parent in prevention cannot be overestimated. Properly addressing the problem involves much more than discussing the dangers of drugs; it involves awareness and responsible action.

Of vital importance is the way we act and live around our children. 85% of all behavior is modeled behavior. Modeling involves much more than not abusing chemicals. Proper expression